DASH
Diet Cookbook
Weight Loss

2 Books in 1 | Dr. Cole's Weight Loss Plan | A Right Way to Kickstart your Body Transformation with Quick and Easy Low Sodium Recipes

(Premium Edition)

By Janeth Cole

Copyright © 2021 Janeth Cole

All rights reserved.

ISBN: 978-1-80312-060-7 (Paperback)

ISBN: 978-1-80312-061-4 (Hardcover)

Table of Contents
1st Book
DASH Diet Cookbook For Women

2nd Book

DASH Diet Cookbook For Athlete

DASH
Diet Cookbook
For Women

Simple Dr. Cole's Meal Plan | Delicious and Affordable Low Sodium Recipes to Weight Loss and Lower Blood Pressure

By Janeth Cole

Chapter 1 -   Introduction

The Dietary Approaches to Stop Hypertension better known as the DASH diet is more than a fad or a trend, it can really make a difference in your health and your appearance. In contrast to other diets, the DASH diet emerged from a group of specialists in 1997 with the goal of reducing high blood pressure. Later, other benefits were found, including the prevention of type II diabetes and help during menopause.

In a research conducted by Valentino, Giovanna, Tagle, Rodrigo, & Acevedo, Mónica (2014) mention the benefits of DASH diet during menopause as a treatment that mitigates the effects caused by the decrease in estrogen production.

Dash Diet Manifesto

The central manifesto of the DASH diet is to reduce dietary sodium to below 2.3 g in regular DASH and 1.5 g in low sodium DASH (equivalent to 3.8 g of salt); increasing consumption of foods rich in potassium, calcium, fiber and magnesium.

In simple terms, it consists of reducing the intake of salt, fats and sugars as much as possible.

What foods can I eat on the DASH diet?

The first thing you should consider is the reduction or elimination of fatty foods, sugary or processed products. You should increase your intake of fresh fruits and vegetables, nuts and seeds, whole grains and dried fruits, fish and lean meat, low-fat or fat-free dairy products. For cooking or frying your food you can opt for olive, coconut or soybean oil.

It also encourages you to stay hydrated by drinking 2 liters of water daily, which also allows you to eliminate excess sodium. Use low-fat cooking techniques such as grilling, broiling, roasting, baking, microwaving or steaming cooking.

Benefits to women

There are many benefits of the DASH diet for all women no matter what age or stage of life you are in, for example: it is your ally during menopause and pre-menopause, helps you lose weight, controls high blood pressure, prevents type II diabetes, reduces the risk of heart disease, controls and improves cholesterol levels, prevents the development of annoying kidney stones. Discover that eating smart is the best way to a fit and healthy body.

Valentino, Giovanna, Tagle, Rodrigo, & Acevedo, Mónica. (2014). Dieta DASH y menopausia: Más allá de los beneficios en hipertensión arterial. *Revista chilena de cardiología*, *33*(3), 215-222. https://dx.doi.org/10.4067/S0718-85602014000300008

DASH DIET BREAKFAST

1) *Cheesy Red Omelette*

Preparation Time: 5 minutes

Cooking Time: 10 minutes

Servings: 4

Nutrition: Calories: 191 Fat: 15g Carbs: 6g Protein: 9g

Ingredients:

- 2 tablespoons olive oil
- 1 medium onion, chopped
- 1 teaspoon garlic, minced
- 2 medium tomatoes, chopped
- 6 large eggs
- ½ cup half and half
- ½ cup feta cheese, crumbled
- ¼ cup dill weed
- Ground black pepper as needed

Directions:

- ❖ Pre-heat your oven to a temperature of 400 degrees Fahrenheit. Take a large sized ovenproof pan and heat up your olive oil over medium-high heat. Toss in the onion, garlic, tomatoes and stir fry them for 4 minutes.
- ❖ While they are being cooked, take a bowl and beat together your eggs, half and half cream and season the mix with some pepper.
- ❖ Pour the mixture into the pan with your vegetables and top it with crumbled feta cheese and dill weed. Cover it with the lid and let it cook for 3 minutes.
- ❖ Place the pan inside your oven and let it bake for 10 minutes. Serve hot.

2) *Apple Warm Oatmeal*

Preparation Time: 10 minutes

Cooking Time: 4 minutes

Servings: 3

Nutrition: calories 200, fat 1g, carbs 12g, protein 10g

Ingredients:

- 3 cups water
- 1 cup steel cut oats
- 1 apple, cored and chopped
- 1 tablespoon cinnamon powder

Directions:

- ❖ In your instant pot, mix water with oats, cinnamon and apple, stir, cover and Cooking Time: on High for 4 minutes.
- ❖ Stir again, divide into bowls and serve for breakfast.
- ❖ Enjoy!

3) *Golden Coco Mix*

Preparation Time: 15 minutes

Cooking Time: 0 minutes

Servings: 6

Nutrition: Calories: 259 Fat: 13g Carbs: 5g Protein: 16g

Ingredients:

- Powdered erythritol as needed
- 1 ½ cups almond milk, unsweetened
- 2 tablespoons vanilla protein powder
- 3 tablespoons Golden Flaxseed meal
- 2 tablespoons coconut flour

Directions:

- ❖ Take a bowl and mix in flaxseed meal, protein powder, coconut flour and mix well. Add mix to saucepan (placed over medium heat).
- ❖ Add almond milk and stir, let the mixture thicken. Add your desired amount of sweetener and serve. Enjoy!

4) *Delicious Agave Rice*

Preparation Time: 10 minutes

Cooking Time: 7 minutes

Servings: 4

Nutrition: calories 192, fat 1g, carbs 20g, protein 4g

Ingredients:

- 1 cup Arborio rice
- 2 cups almond milk
- 1 cup coconut milk
- 1/3 cup agave nectar
- 2 teaspoons vanilla extract
- ¼ cup coconut flakes, toasted

Directions:

- ❖ Set your instant pot on simmer mode, add almond and coconut milk and bring to a boil.
- ❖ Add agave nectar and rice, stir, cover and Cooking Time: on High for 5 minutes.
- ❖ Add vanilla and coconut, stir, divide into bowls and serve warm.
- ❖ Enjoy!

5) *Italian Feta Breakfast Eggs*

Preparation Time: 5 minutes

Cooking Time: 15 minutes

Servings: 12

Nutrition: Calories: 106 Fat: 8g Carbs: 2g Protein: 7g

Ingredients:

- 2 tablespoons of unsalted butter (replace with canola oil for full effect)
- ½ cup of chopped up scallions
- 1 cup of crumbled feta cheese
- 8 large sized eggs
- 2/3 cup of milk
- ½ teaspoon of dried Italian seasoning
- Freshly ground black pepper as needed
- Cooking oil spray

Directions:

- ❖ Pre-heat your oven to 400 degrees Fahrenheit. Take a 3-4 ounce muffin pan and grease with cooking oil. Take a non-stick pan and place it over medium heat.
- ❖ Add butter and allow the butter to melt. Add half of the scallions and stir fry. Keep them to the side. Take a medium-sized bowl and add eggs, Italian seasoning and milk and whisk well.
- ❖ Add the stir fried scallions and feta cheese and mix. Season with pepper. Pour the mix into the muffin tin. Transfer the muffin tin to your oven and bake for 15 minutes. Serve with a sprinkle of scallions.

6) Cinnamon Pumpkin Oatmeal with Vanilla Flavour

Preparation Time: 10 minutes

Cooking Time: 3 minutes

Servings: 6

Nutrition: calories 173, fat 1g, carbs 20g, protein 6g

Ingredients:

- 4 and ½ cups water
- 1 and ½ cups steel cut oats
- 2 teaspoons cinnamon powder
- 1 teaspoon vanilla extract
- 1 teaspoon allspice
- 1 and ½ cup pumpkin puree
- ¼ cup pecans, chopped

Directions:

- ❖ In your instant pot, mix water with oats, cinnamon, vanilla allspice and pumpkin puree, stir, cover and Cooking Time: on High for 3 minutes.
- ❖ Divide into bowls, stir again, cool down and serve with pecans on top.
- ❖ Enjoy!

7) Button Mushroom Omelette

Preparation Time: 5 minutes

Cooking Time: 15 minutes

Servings: 4

Nutrition: Calories: 189 Fat: 13g Carbs: 6g Protein: 12g

Ingredients:

- 2 tablespoons of butter (replace with canola oil for full effect)
- 1 chopped up medium-sized onion
- 2 minced cloves of garlic
- 1 cup of coarsely chopped baby rocket tomato
- 1 cup of sliced button mushrooms
- 6 large pieces of eggs
- ½ cup of skim milk
- 1 teaspoon of dried rosemary
- Ground black pepper as needed

Directions:

- ❖ Pre-heat your oven to 400 degrees Fahrenheit. Take a large oven-proof pan and place it over medium-heat. Heat up some oil.
- ❖ Stir fry your garlic, onion for about 2 minutes. Add the mushroom, rosemary and rockets and cook for 3 minutes. Take a medium-sized bowl and beat your eggs alongside the milk.
- ❖ Season it with some pepper. Pour the egg mixture into your pan with the vegetables and sprinkle some Parmesan.
- ❖ Reduce the heat to low and cover with the lid. Let it cook for 3 minutes. Transfer the pan into your oven and bake for 10 minutes until fully settled.
- ❖ Reduce the heat to low and cover with your lid. Let it cook for 3 minutes. Transfer the pan into your oven and then bake for another 10 minutes. Serve hot.

8) Easy Tofu Bowl

Preparation Time: 10 minutes

Cooking Time: 10 minutes

Servings:4

Nutrition: calories 172, fat 7g, carbs 20g, protein 6g

Ingredients:

- 1 pound extra firm tofu, cubed
- 1 cup sweet potato, chopped
- 3 garlic cloves, minced
- 2 tablespoons sesame seeds
- 1 yellow onion, chopped
- 2 teaspoons sesame seed oil
- 1 carrot, chopped
- 1 tablespoon tamari
- 1 tablespoon rice vinegar
- 2 cups snow peas, halved
- 1/3 cup veggie stock
- 2 tablespoons red pepper sauce
- 2 tablespoons scallions, chopped
- 2 tablespoons tahini paste

Directions:

- ❖ Set your instant pot on sauté mode, add oil, heat it up, add sweet potato, onion and carrots, stir and Cooking Time: for 2 minutes.
- ❖ Add garlic, half of the sesame seeds, tofu, vinegar, tamari and stock, stir and Cooking Time: for 2 minutes more.
- ❖ Cover pot and Cooking Time: on High for 3 minutes more.
- ❖ Add peas, the rest of the sesame seeds, green onions, tahini paste and pepper sauce, stir, cover and Cooking Time: on Low for 1 minutes more.
- ❖ Divide into bowls and serve for breakfast.
- ❖ Enjoy!

9) Canned Beans and Tomato Breads

Preparation Time: 5 minutes

Cooking Time: 15 minutes

Servings: 4

Nutrition: Calories 382 Fat: 1.8g Carbs: 66g Protein: 28.5g

Ingredients:

- 1 ½ tbsp olive oil
- 1 tomato, cubed
- 1 garlic clove, minced
- 1 red onion, chopped
- ¼ cup parsley, chopped
- 15 oz. canned fava beans, drained and rinsed
- ¼ cup lemon juice
- Black pepper to the taste
- 4 whole-wheat pita bread pockets

Directions:

- ❖ Heat a pan with the oil over medium heat, add the onion, stir, and sauté for 5 minutes. Add the rest of the ingredients, stir, and cook for 10 minutes more
- ❖ Stuff the pita pockets with this mix and serve for breakfast.

10) Black Olives and Feta Bread

Preparation Time: 1 hour and 40 minutes

Cooking Time: 30 minutes

Servings: 10

Nutrition: Calories 251 Fat: 7.3g Carbs: 39.7g Protein: 6.7g

Ingredients:

- 4 cups whole-wheat flour
- 3 tbsps. oregano, chopped
- 2 tsps. dry yeast
- ¼ cup olive oil
- 1 ½ cups black olives, pitted and sliced
- 1 cup of water
- ½ cup feta cheese, crumbled

Directions:

- ❖ In a bowl, mix the flour with the water, the yeast, and the oil. Stir and knead your dough very well. Put the dough in a bowl, cover with plastic wrap, and keep in a warm place for 1 hour.
- ❖ Divide the dough into 2 bowls and stretch each ball well. Add the rest of the ingredients to each ball and tuck them inside. Knead the dough well again.
- ❖ Flatten the balls a bit and leave them aside for 40 minutes more. Transfer the balls to a baking sheet lined with parchment paper, make a small slit in each, and bake at 425F for 30 minutes.
- ❖ Serve the bread as a Mediterranean breakfast.

11) Lentils and Mushroom Burgers

Preparation Time: 10 minutes

Cooking Time: 30 minutes

Servings: 4

Nutrition: calories 140, fat 3g, carbs 14g, protein 13g

Ingredients:

- 1 cup mushrooms, chopped
- 2 teaspoons ginger, grated
- 1 cup yellow onion, chopped
- 1 cup red lentils
- 1 sweet potato, chopped
- 2 and ½ cups veggie stock
- ¼ cup hemp seeds
- ¼ cup parsley, chopped
- 1 tablespoon curry powder
- ¼ cup cilantro, chopped
- 1 cup quick oats
- 4 tablespoons rice flour

Direction:

- ❖ Set your instant pot on sauté mode, add onion, mushrooms and ginger, stir and sauté for 2 minutes.
- ❖ Add lentils, stock and sweet potatoes, stir, cover and Cooking Time: on High for 6 minutes.
- ❖ Leave this mixture aside to cool down, mash using a potato masher, add parsley, hemp, curry powder, cilantro, oats and rice flour and stir well.
- ❖ Shape 8 patties out of this mix, arrange them all on a lined baking sheet, introduce in the oven at 375 degrees F and bake for 10 minutes on each side.
- ❖ Divide between plates and serve for breakfast.
- ❖ Enjoy!

12) Cheesy Baked Potato

Preparation Time: 10 minutes

Cooking Time: 1 hour and 10 minutes

Servings: 8

Nutrition: Calories 476 Fat: 16.8g Carbs: 68.8g Protein: 13.9g

Ingredients:

- 2 pounds sweet potatoes, peeled and cubed
- ¼ cup olive oil + a drizzle
- 7 oz. feta cheese, crumbled
- 1 yellow onion, chopped
- 2 eggs, whisked
- ¼ cup almond milk
- 1 tbsp. herbs de Provence
- A pinch of black pepper
- 6 phyllo sheets
- 1 tbsp. parmesan, grated

Directions:

- ❖ In a bowl, combine the potatoes with half of the oil, and pepper, toss, spread on a baking sheet lined with parchment paper, and roast at 400F for 25 minutes.
- ❖ Meanwhile, heat a pan with half of the remaining oil over medium heat, add the onion, and sauté for 5 minutes.
- ❖ In a bowl, combine the eggs with the milk, feta, herbs, pepper, onion, sweet potatoes, and the rest of the oil and toss.
- ❖ Arrange the phyllo sheets in a tart pan and brush them with a drizzle of oil. Add the sweet potato mix and spread it well into the pan.
- ❖ Sprinkle the parmesan on top and bake covered with tin foil at 350F for 20 minutes. Remove the tin foil, bake the tart for 20 minutes more, cool it down, slice, and serve for breakfast.

13) Breakfast Walnuts Quinoa

Preparation Time: 5 minutes

Cooking Time: 0 minutes

Servings: 4

Nutrition: Calories 284 Fat: 14.3g Carbs: 15.4g Protein: 4.4g

Ingredients:

- 2 cups almond milk
- 2 cups quinoa, already cooked
- ½ tsp cinnamon powder
- 1 tbsp. honey
- 1 cup blueberries
- ¼ cup walnuts, chopped

Directions:

- ❖ In a bowl, mix the quinoa with the milk and the rest of the ingredients, toss, divide into smaller bowls and serve for breakfast

14) Vegetables Wraps with Soy Sauce

Preparation Time: 10 minutes

Cooking Time: 15 minutes

Servings: 6

Nutrition: calories 100, fat 2g, carbs 9g, protein 3g

Ingredients:

- 1 tablespoon olive oil
- 1 cup mushrooms, chopped
- 1 and ½ cups cabbage, chopped
- ½ cup carrots, grated
- 1 and ½ cups water
- 2 tablespoons soy sauce
- 1 teaspoon ginger, grated
- 1 tablespoon rice wine vinegar
- 1 teaspoon sesame oil
- 12 vegan dumpling wrappers

Directions:

- ❖ Set your instant pot on sauté mode, add olive oil, heat it up, add mushrooms, stir and Cooking Time: for 2 minutes.
- ❖ Add carrot, cabbage, soy sauce and vinegar, stir and Cooking Time: for 3 minutes more.
- ❖ Add sesame oil and ginger, stir and transfer everything to a bowl.
- ❖ Arrange all wrappers on a working surface, divide veggie mix, wrap them and seal with some water.
- ❖ Add the water to your instant pot, add steamer basket, add dumplings inside, cover pot and Cooking Time: on High for 7 minutes.
- ❖ Divide between plates and serve for breakfast.
- ❖ Enjoy!

15) Brown Rice and Chickpeas Breakfast Bowl

Preparation Time: Breakfast Rice Bowl

Cooking Time: 30 minutes

Servings: 4

Nutrition: calories 292, fat 4g, carbs 9g, protein 10g

Ingredients:

- 1 tablespoon olive oil
- 2 tablespoons chana masala
- 1 red onion, chopped
- 1 tablespoon ginger, grated
- 1 tablespoon garlic, minced
- 1 cup chickpeas
- 3 cups water
- A pinch of black pepper
- 14 ounces tomatoes, chopped
- 1 and ½ cups brown rice

Directions:

- ❖ Set your instant pot on sauté mode, add the oil, heat it up, add onion, stir and Cooking Time: for 7 minutes.
- ❖ Add pepper, chana masala, ginger and garlic, stir and Cooking Time: for 1
- ❖ minute more.
- ❖ Add tomatoes, chickpeas, rice and water, stir, cover and Cooking Time: on High for 20 minutes.
- ❖ Stir one more time, divide into bowls and serve for breakfast.
- ❖ Enjoy!

16) Sauté Vegan Millet

Preparation Time: 10 minutes

Cooking Time: 16 minutes

Servings: 4

Nutrition: calories 172, fat 3g, carbs 19g, protein 5g

Ingredients:

- 1 cup millet
- ½ cup oyster mushrooms, chopped
- 2 garlic cloves, minced
- ½ cup green lentils
- ½ cup bok choy, chopped
- 2 and ¼ cups veggie stock
- 1 cup yellow onion, chopped
- 1 cup asparagus, chopped
- 1 tablespoon lemon juice
- ¼ cup parsley and chives, chopped

Directions:

- ❖ Set your instant pot on sauté mode, heat it up, add garlic, onion and mushrooms, stir and Cooking Time: for 2 minutes.
- ❖ Add lentils and millet, stir and Cooking Time: for a few seconds more.
- ❖ Add stock, stir, cover and Cooking Time: on High for 10 minutes.
- ❖ Add asparagus and bok choy, stir, cover and leave everything aside for 3 minutes.
- ❖ Add parsley and chives and lemon juice, stir, divide into bowls and serve for breakfast.
- ❖ Enjoy!

17) Black Navel Salad

Preparation Time: 5 minutes

Cooking Time: 0 minutes

Servings: 4

Nutrition: Calories 97 Fat: 9.1g Carbs: 3.7g Protein: 1.9g

Ingredients:

- 1 tbsp. balsamic vinegar
- 2 garlic cloves, minced
- 1 tsp. Dijon mustard
- 2 tbsps. olive oil
- 1 tbsp. lemon juice
- Black pepper to taste
- ½ cup black olives, pitted and chopped
- 1 tbsp. parsley, chopped
- 7 cups baby spinach
- 2 endives, shredded
- 3 medium navel oranges, peeled and cut into segments
- 2 bulbs fennel, shredded

Directions:

- ❖ In a salad bowl, combine the spinach with the endives, oranges, fennel, and the rest of the ingredients, toss and serve for breakfast.

18) Almond Pearls Pudding

Preparation Time: 10 minutes

Cooking Time: 8 minutes

Servings: 4

Nutrition: calories 187, fat 3g, fiber 1g, carbs 18g, protein 3g

Ingredients:

- 1/3 cup tapioca pearls
- ½ cup water
- 1 and ¼ cups almond milk
- ½ cup stevia
- Zest from ½ lemon, grated

Directions:

- ❖ In a heatproof bowl, mix tapioca with almond milk, stevia and lemon zest and stir well.
- ❖ Add the water to your instant pot, add steamer basket, and heatproof bowl inside, cover and Cooking Time: on High for 8 minutes.
- ❖ Stir your pudding and serve for breakfast.
- ❖ Enjoy!

19) Awesome Brakfast Muesli

Preparation Time: 15 minutes

Cooking Time: 20 minutes

Servings: 8

Nutrition: Calories 250 Fat: 10g Carbs: 36g Protein: 7g

Ingredients:

- 3 ½ cups rolled oats
- ½ cup wheat bran
- ½ tsp ground cinnamon
- ½ cup sliced almonds
- ¼ cup raw pecans, coarsely chopped
- ¼ cup raw pepitas (shelled pumpkin seeds)
- ½ cup unsweetened coconut flakes
- ¼ cup dried apricots, coarsely chopped
- ¼ cup dried cherries

Directions:

- ❖ Take a medium bowl and combine the oats, wheat bran and cinnamon. Stir well. Place the mixture onto a baking sheet.
- ❖ Next place the almonds, pecans, and pepitas onto another baking sheet and toss. Pop both trays into the oven and heat to 350°F. Bake for 10-12 minutes. Remove from the oven and pop to one side.
- ❖ Leave the nuts to cool but take the one with the oats, sprinkle with the coconut, and pop back into the oven for 5 minutes more. Remove and leave to cool.
- ❖ Find a large bowl and combine the contents of both trays then stir well to combine. Throw in the apricots and cherries and stir well. Pop into an airtight container until required.

20) Delicious Kamut Salad with Walnuts

Preparation Time: 10 minutes

Cooking Time: 15 minutes

Servings: 6

Nutrition: calories 125, fat 6g, fiber 2g, carbs 4g, protein 3g

Ingredients:

- 2 cups water
- 1 cup kamut grains, soaked for 12 hours, drained and mixed with some lemon juice
- 1 teaspoon sunflower oil
- 4 ounces arugula
- 2 blood oranges, peeled and cut into medium segments
- 1 tablespoon olive oil
- 3 ounces walnuts, chopped

Directions:

- ❖ In your instant pot, mix kamut grains with sunflower oil and the water, stir, cover and Cooking Time: on High for 15 minutes.
- ❖ Drain kamut, transfer to a bowl, add a
- ❖ pinch of salt, arugula, orange segments, oil and walnuts, toss well and serve for breakfast.
- ❖ Enjoy!

DASH DIET RICE, GRAIN & PASTA RECIPES

21) Pasta with Delicious Spanish Salsa

Preparation Time: 15 minutes

Cooking Time:

Servings: 2

Nutrition: Carbs: 69g Protein: 12.7g Fats: 2.3g Calories: 364

Ingredients:
- Spaghetti : 160g
- Red onion: ½ roughly chopped
- Green pepper: 1 chopped
- Cherry tomatoes:250g
- Tabasco: a good dash
- Garlic: ½ clove
- Vinegar: 1 tbsp
- Basi l a small bunch

Directions:
- ❖ Cooking Time: pasta as per packet instructions
- ❖ In the meanwhile, take a blender and add tomatoes, garlic, onion, and pepper, and blend
- ❖ Add in Tabasco and vinegar and combine well
- ❖ Add the sauce to the paste
- ❖ Top with basil and serve

22) Penne with Zucchini and Wine

Preparation Time: 15 minutes

Cooking Time: 30 minutes

Servings: 6

Nutrition: Calories: 340 Fat: 6.2g Protein: 8.0g Carbs: 66.8g

Ingredients:
- 1 large zucchini, diced
- 1 large butternut squash, peeled and diced
- 1 large yellow onion, chopped
- 2 tablespoons extra-virgin olive oil
- 1 teaspoon paprika
- ½ teaspoon garlic powder
- ½ teaspoon freshly ground black pepper
- 1 pound (454 g) whole-grain penne
- ½ cup dry white wine
- 2 tablespoons grated Parmesan cheese

Directions:
- ❖ Preheat the oven to 400°F (205°C). Line a baking sheet with aluminum foil. Combine the zucchini, butternut squash, and onion in a large bowl.
- ❖ Drizzle with olive oil and sprinkle with paprika, garlic powder, and ground black pepper. Toss to coat well.
- ❖ Spread the vegetables in the single layer on the baking sheet, then roast in the preheated oven for 25 minutes or until the vegetables are tender.
- ❖ Meanwhile, bring a pot of water to a boil, then add the penne and cook for 14 minutes or until al dente. Drain the penne through a colander.
- ❖ Transfer ½ cup of roasted vegetables in a food processor, then pour in the dry white wine. Pulse until smooth.
- ❖ Pour the puréed vegetables in a nonstick skillet and cook with penne over medium-high heat for a few minutes to heat through.
- ❖ Transfer the penne with the purée on a large serving plate, then spread the remaining roasted vegetables and Parmesan on top before serving.

23) Gochujang and Carrot Spaghetti with Coriander

Preparation Time: 45 minutes

Cooking Time:

Servings: 2

Nutrition: Carbs: 52.5g Protein: 10.9g Fats: 15.5g Calories: 404

Ingredients:
- Spaghetti: 2 cups
- Olive oil: 2 tbsp
- Cauliflower: 2 cups cut in big florets
- Gochujang: 2 tbsp
- Rice vinegar: 1 tbsp
- Sliced red pepper: 1 cup sliced
- Carrot: 2 sliced
- Pepper: as per your taste
- Coriander: 1⁄2 cup chopped

Directions:
- ❖ Cooking Time: spaghetti as per packet instructions
- ❖ Preheat the oven 200C
- ❖ Add cauliflowers to the baking sheet and sprinkle seasoning and brush with olive oil
- ❖ Roast for 25 minutes till it turns golden and soft
- ❖ Remove from oven and brush with gochujang and Cooking Time: in the oven again for 10 minutes
- ❖ Add to the bowl and mix with carrots and red bell pepper
- ❖ Season with coriander, and pepper and pour vinegar from top
- ❖ Spread spaghetti on the serving tray and top with the cauliflower

24) Spinach Cheesy Pasta

Preparation Time: 15 minutes

Cooking Time: 14-16 minutes

Servings: 4

Nutrition: Calories: 262 Fat: 4.0g Protein: 15.0g Carbs: 51.0g

Ingredients:

- 8 ounces (227 g) uncooked penne
- 1 tablespoon extra-virgin olive oil
- 2 garlic cloves, minced
- ¼ teaspoon crushed red pepper
- 2 cups chopped fresh flat-leaf parsley, including stems
- 5 cups loosely packed baby spinach
- ¼ teaspoon ground nutmeg
- ¼ teaspoon freshly ground black pepper
- 1/3 cup Castelvetrano olives, pitted and sliced
- 1/3 cup grated Parmesan cheese

Directions:

- ❖ In a large stockpot of salted water, cook the pasta for about 8 to 10 minutes. Drain the pasta and reserve ¼ cup of the cooking liquid.
- ❖ Meanwhile, heat the olive oil in a large skillet over medium heat. Add the garlic and red pepper and cook for 30 seconds, stirring constantly.
- ❖ Add the parsley and cook for 1 minute, stirring constantly. Add the spinach, nutmeg and pepper, and cook for 3 minutes, stirring occasionally, or until the spinach is wilted.
- ❖ Add the cooked pasta and the reserved ¼ cup cooking liquid to the skillet. Stir in the olives and cook for about 2 minutes, or until most of the pasta water has been absorbed.
- ❖ Remove from the heat and stir in the cheese before serving.

25) Chickpeas Tomato Pasta with Tamari

Preparation Time: 30 minutes

Cooking Time:

Servings: 2

Nutrition: Carbs: 54g Protein: 14.6g Fats: 18g Calories: 442

Ingredients:

- Pasta: 1 cup cooked
- Chickpeas: 1 cup rinsed and drained well
- Onion: 1 cup finely diced
- Tomato: 2 cups diced
- Lemon juice: 2 tbsp
- Kale: 1 cup
- Olive oil: 2 tbsp
- Tamari: 1 tbsp
- Coriander: 2 tbsp chopped
- Garlic: 1 clove crushed

Directions:

- ❖ Cooking Time: pasta as per packet instructions
- ❖ Add garlic, lemon juice, tamari, and olive oil in a bowl and whisk
- ❖ Take a serving bowl and combine kale, pasta, chickpeas, onion, tomatoes, and the sauce you made
- ❖ Add coriander from the top and serve

26) Italian Tricolor Pasta

Preparation Time: 5 minutes

Cooking Time: 25 minutes

Servings: 6

Nutrition: Calories: 147 Fat: 3.0g Protein: 16.0g Carbs: 17.0g

Ingredients:

- 8 ounces (227 g) uncooked small pasta, like orecchiette (little ears) or farfalle (bow ties)
- 1½ pounds (680 g) fresh asparagus, ends trimmed and stalks chopped into 1-inch pieces
- 1½ cups grape tomatoes, halved
- 2 tablespoons extra-virgin olive oil
- ¼ teaspoon freshly ground black pepper
- 2 cups fresh Mozzarella, drained and cut into bite-size pieces (about 8 ounces / 227 g)
- 1/3 cup torn fresh basil leaves
- 2 tablespoons balsamic vinegar

Directions:

- ❖ Preheat the oven to 400°F (205°C). In a large stockpot of salted water, cook the pasta for about 8 to 10 minutes. Drain and reserve about ¼ cup of the cooking liquid.
- ❖ Meanwhile, in a large bowl, toss together the asparagus, tomatoes, oil and pepper. Spread the mixture onto a large, rimmed baking sheet and bake in the oven for 15 minutes, stirring twice during cooking.
- ❖ Remove the vegetables from the oven and add the cooked pasta to the baking sheet. Mix with a few tablespoons of cooking liquid to help the sauce become smoother and the saucy vegetables stick to the pasta.
- ❖ Gently mix in the Mozzarella and basil. Drizzle with the balsamic vinegar. Serve from the baking sheet or pour the pasta into a large bowl.

27) Fusilli with Juicy Cauliflowers

Preparation Time: 20 minutes

Cooking Time:

Servings: 2

Nutrition: Carbs: 21.6g Protein: 4.85g Fats: 7.9g Calories: 172

Ingredients:
- Fusilli: 1 cup cooked
- Cauliflower: 1 cup roughly chopped
- Garlic: 2 cloves thinly sliced
- Olive oil: 1 tbsp
- Chili flakes: 1 tsp
- Pepper: as per your taste
- Lemon: 1 juice and zest

Directions:
- ❖ Cooking Time: the pasta as per the packet instruction
- ❖ Add cauliflower when the pasta is about to be done
- ❖ Drain but keep one cup of the water
- ❖ Take a large pan and heat oil
- ❖ Add in garlic and Cooking Time: for two minutes
- ❖ Add in chili and Cooking Time: for a minutes
- ❖ Add pasta, lemon juice and zest, pepper, and cauliflower with the pasta water
- ❖ Mix everything well and serve

28) Shrimp Fettuccine with Black Pepper

Preparation Time: 15 minutes

Cooking Time: 15 minutes

Servings: 4-6

Nutrition: Calories: 615 Fat: 17.0g Protein: 33.0g Carbs: 89.0g

Ingredients:
- 8 ounces (227 g) fettuccine pasta
- ¼ cup extra-virgin olive oil
- 3 tablespoons garlic, minced
- 1 pound (454 g) large shrimp, peeled and deveined
- 1/3 cup lemon juice
- 1 tablespoon lemon zest
- ½ teaspoon freshly ground black pepper

Directions:
- ❖ Bring a large pot of water to a boil. Add the fettuccine and cook for 8 minutes. Reserve ½ cup of the cooking liquid and drain the pasta.
- ❖ In a large saucepan over medium heat, heat the olive oil. Add the garlic and sauté for 1 minute.
- ❖ Add the shrimp to the saucepan and cook each side for 3 minutes. Remove the shrimp from the pan and set aside.
- ❖ Add the remaining ingredients to the saucepan. Stir in the cooking liquid. Add the pasta and toss together to evenly coat the pasta.
- ❖ Transfer the pasta to a serving dish and serve topped with the cooked shrimp.

29) Spiced Kidney Pasta with Cilantro

Preparation Time: 30 minutes

Cooking Time:

Servings: 4

Nutrition: Carbs: 41.98g Protein: 9.3g Fats: 8.4g Calories: 274

Ingredients:
- Pasta: 2 cups (after cooking
- Onion: 1 chopped
- Garlic: 1 ½ tsp minced
- Cumin: 1 tsp
- Frozen corn: 1 cup
- Cayenne pepper: ¼ tsp
- Kidney beans: 1 cup drained and rinsed
- Fresh cilantro: 2 tsp
- Lemon juice: 3 tbsp
- Cooking oil: 2 tbsp

Directions:
- ❖ Cooking Time: pasta as per packet instructions
- ❖ Take a saucepan and heat oil in it
- ❖ Add garlic and onion to it and make them tender
- ❖ Add cayenne pepper, and cumin
- ❖ Now add corns and beans and mix well
- ❖ Cover and Cooking Time: for 5 minutes
- ❖ Add in pasta and stir and remove from heat after 5 minutes
- ❖ Pour lemon juice on top
- ❖ Garnish with cilantro and serve

30) Classic Grandma's Pasta

Preparation Time: 15 minutes

Cooking Time: 25 minutes

Servings: 4

Nutrition: Calories 500 Fat 18.3 g Carbohydrates 69.7 g Protein 16.2 g

Ingredients:
- 1 pack of 16 angel hair pasta
- 1/4 cup of olive oil
- 1/2 onion, minced
- 4 cloves of chopped garlic
- 2 cups of Roma tomatoes, diced
- 2 tablespoons balsamic vinegar
- 1 low-sodium chicken broth
- ground red pepper
- freshly ground black pepper to taste
- 1/4 cup grated Parmesan cheese
- 2 tablespoons chopped fresh basil

Directions:
- ❖ Bring a large pot of water to a boil. Add pasta and cook for 8 minutes or until al dente; drain.
- ❖ Pour the olive oil in a large deep pan over high heat. Fry onions and garlic until light brown. Lower the heat to medium and add tomatoes, vinegar, and chicken stock; simmer for about 8 minutes.
- ❖ Stir in the red pepper, black pepper, basil, and cooked pasta and mix well with the sauce. Simmer for about 5 minutes and serve garnished with grated cheese.

31) Red Lentils Spaghetti with Herbs

Preparation Time: :45 minutes

Cooking Time:

Servings: 2

Nutrition: Carbs: 33.33g Protein: 13.3g Fats: 15.1g Calories: 335.2

Ingredients:

- Spaghetti: 1 cup cooked
- Red lentils: 1 cup
- Potato: 1 cup diced
- Crushed tomatoes: 2 cups
- Onion: 1 diced
- Ginger: 1 tbsp paste
- Garlic: 1 tbsp paste
- Vegetable oil: 2 tbsp
- Water: 4 cups
- Italian herb seasoning: 1 tbsp
- Pepper: as per your taste

Directions:

- ❖ Cooking Time: spaghetti as per packet instructions
- ❖ Take a large saucepan and heat oil on a medium flame
- ❖ Add onion and ginger and garlic paste and sauté for 3-4 minutes
- ❖ Pour water and bring to boil
- ❖ Add lentils, potatoes and bring to boil
- ❖ Lower the heat to medium and Cooking Time: for 20 minutes with partial cover
- ❖ Now add crushed tomatoes to the lentils along with Italian herb seasoning and pepper
- ❖ Cooking Time: on low flame for 15 minutes
- ❖ Add the mixture to the high-speed blender to make a puree
- ❖ Add in spaghetti pasta and mix well
- ❖ Add pepper to augment the taste

32) Spicy Shrimp Pasta with Bay Scallops

Preparation Time: 15 minutes

Cooking Time: 55 minutes

Servings: 8

Nutrition: Calories 335 Fat 8.9 g Carbs 46.3 g Protein 18.7 g

Ingredients:

- 4 tablespoons olive oil, divided
- 6 cloves of garlic, crushed
- 3 cups peeled whole tomatoes with liquid, chopped
- 1 teaspoon crushed red pepper flakes
- 1 packet of linguine pasta
- 8 grams of small shrimp, peeled
- 8 grams of bay scallops
- 1 tablespoon of chopped fresh parsley

Directions:

- ❖ Heat 2 tablespoons of olive oil and sauté garlic over medium heat. When the garlic starts to sizzle, pour in the tomatoes.
- ❖ Season with red pepper. Bring to boil. Reduce the heat and simmer for 30 minutes, stirring occasionally.
- ❖ Meanwhile, boil a large pan with lightly salted water. Cook pasta for about 8 to 10 minutes or until al dente; drain.
- ❖ Heat the remaining 2 tablespoons of olive oil in a large frying pan over high heat. Add shrimps and scallops. Cook for about 2 minutes stirring regularly, or until the shrimp turn pink.
- ❖ Add the shrimp and scallops to the tomato mixture and stir in the parsley. Bake for 3 to 4 minutes or until the sauce starts to bubble. Serve the sauce on the pasta.

33) Italian Pasta e Fagioli

Preparation Time: 30 minutes

Cooking Time:

Servings: 2

Nutrition: Carbs: 39.2g Protein: 11.3g Fats: 8.2g Calories: 272

Ingredients:

- Pasta: 1 cup (after cooking
- Olive oil: 1 tbsp
- Beans: 1 cup can rinsed and drained
- Garlic: 2 cloves minced
- Tomato paste: ¼ cup
- Red onion: 1 small diced
- Red chili flakes: 1 tsp
- Black pepper: ½ tsp
- Parsley: ½ cup

Directions:

- ❖ Cooking Time: pasta as per packet instructions
- ❖ Take a saucepan and heat oil in it
- ❖ Add minced garlic and onion to it and
- ❖ make them tender
- ❖ Add beans, pepper, tomato paste, and red chili flakes and mix well
- ❖ Add cooked pasta and stir
- ❖ Lower the heat and cover and Cooking Time: for 5 minutes and then remove from heat
- ❖ Sprinkle parsley on top and serve

34) Penne with Vodka Cream

Preparation Time: 15 minutes

Cooking Time: 25 minutes

Servings: 8

Nutrition: Calories 435 Fat 18.4 g Carbs 52.7 g Protein 13.3 g

Ingredients:

- 1-pound uncooked penne
- 1/4 cup extra virgin olive oil
- 4 cloves finely chopped garlic
- 1/2 teaspoon crushed red pepper flakes
- 1 can of crushed tomatoes
- 2 tablespoons of vodka
- 1/2 cup thick whipped cream
- 1/4 cup chopped fresh parsley
- 2 (3.5 ounces) sweet Italian sausage links

Directions:

- ❖ Bring a large pan of water to a boil. Put the pasta and cook for 8 to 10 minutes or until al dente; drain.
- ❖ Heat the oil in a large frying pan over medium heat. Remove the casing from the sausage and add it to the pan.
- ❖ Cook by browning the meat, add garlic and red pepper and cook, stirring until the garlic is golden brown. Add tomatoes and boil. Lower the heat and simmer for 15 minutes.
- ❖ Add vodka and cream and bring to a boil. Reduce the heat and add the pasta, mix for 1 minute. Stir in the fresh parsley and serve!

35) Macaroni with Cherry and Peas

Preparation Time: 40 minutes

Cooking Time:

Servings: 2

Nutrition: Carbs: 37.5g Protein: 8.9g Fats: 15.4g Calories: 320

Ingredients:

- Macaroni: 1 cup (after cooking
- Frozen peas: 1 cup rinsed and drained
- Cherry tomatoes: 1 cup diced
- Onions: 1 chopped
- Garlic: 2 cloves
- Vinegar: 3 tbsp
- Olive oil: 2 tbsp
- Tahini: 2 tbsp
- Pepper: as per your taste
- Spring onion greens: 3 tbsp chopped

Directions:

- ❖ Take a pan and heat oil
- ❖ Add onion and sauté for 5 minutes
- ❖ Add tomatoes and whole garlic cloves and sauté for 5 minutes and stir
- ❖ Add in vinegar, tahini, and a lot of pepper
- ❖ Cooking Time: macaroni as per packet instructions and add peas at the end
- ❖ Drain the pasta but keep 2 tablespoons of water and add to tomatoes
- ❖ Add the tomato mixture to the blender and blend
- ❖ Combine pasta and tomato mixture
- ❖ Serve with spring onions on top

36) Brown Rice with Lentils in Veggie Broth

Preparation Time: 5 minutes

Cooking Time: 25 minutes

Servings: 4

Nutrition: Calories: 230 Fat: 8g Carbs: 34g Protein: 8g

Ingredients:

- 2¼ cups low-sodium or no-salt-added vegetable broth
- ½ cup uncooked brown or green lentils
- ½ cup uncooked instant brown rice
- ½ cup diced carrots (about 1 carrot)
- ½ cup diced celery (about 1 stalk)
- 1 (2.25-ounce) can sliced olives, drained (about ½ cup)
- ¼ cup diced red onion (about 1/8 onion)
- ¼ cup chopped fresh curly-leaf parsley
- 1½ tablespoons extra-virgin olive oil
- 1 tablespoon freshly squeezed lemon juice (from about ½ small lemon)
- 1 garlic clove, minced (about ½ teaspoon)
- ¼ teaspoon freshly ground black pepper

Directions:

- ❖ In a medium saucepan over high heat, bring the broth and lentils to a boil, cover, and lower the heat to medium-low. Cook for 8 minutes.
- ❖ Raise the heat to medium, and stir in the rice. Cover the pot and cook the mixture for 15 minutes, or until the liquid is absorbed. Remove the pot from the heat and let it sit, covered, for 1 minute, then stir.
- ❖ While the lentils and rice are cooking, mix together the carrots, celery, olives, onion, and parsley in a large serving bowl.
- ❖ In a small bowl, whisk together the oil, lemon juice, garlic and pepper. Set aside. When the lentils and rice are cooked, add them to the serving bowl.
- ❖ Pour the dressing on top, and mix everything together. Serve warm or cold, or store in a sealed container in the refrigerator for up to 7 days.

37) Golden Rice with Pistachios

Preparation Time: 5 minutes

Cooking Time: 15 minutes

Servings: 6

Nutrition: Calories: 320 Fat: 7g Carbs: 61g Protein: 6g

Ingredients:

- 1 tablespoon extra-virgin olive oil
- 1 cup chopped onion (about ½ medium onion)
- ½ cup shredded carrot (about 1 medium carrot)
- 1 teaspoon ground cumin
- ½ teaspoon ground cinnamon
- 2 cups instant brown rice
- 1¾ cups 100% orange juice
- ¼ cup water
- 1 cup golden raisins
- ½ cup shelled pistachios
- Chopped fresh chives (optional)

Directions:

- ❖ In a medium saucepan over medium-high heat, heat the oil. Add the onion and cook for 5 minutes, stirring frequently.
- ❖ Add the carrot, cumin, and cinnamon, and cook for 1 minute, stirring frequently. Stir in the rice, orange juice, and water.
- ❖ Bring to a boil, cover, then lower the heat to medium-low. Simmer for 7 minutes, or until the rice is cooked through and the liquid is absorbed. Stir in the raisins, pistachios, and chives (if using) and serve.

38) Quinoa and Veggie Mix Salad

Preparation Time: 15 minutes

Cooking Time: 15 minutes

Servings: 4

Nutrition: Calories: 366 Fat: 11.1g Protein: 15.5g Carbs: 55.6g

Ingredients:

- 1 cup red dry quinoa, rinsed and drained
- 2 cups low-sodium vegetable soup
- 2 cups fresh spinach
- 2 cups finely shredded red cabbage
- 1 (15-ounce / 425-g) can chickpeas, drained and rinsed
- 1 ripe avocado, thinly sliced
- 1 cup shredded carrots
- 1 red bell pepper, thinly sliced
- 4 tablespoons Mango Sauce
- ½ cup fresh cilantro, chopped
- Mango Sauce:
- 1 mango, diced
- ¼ cup fresh lime juice
- ½ teaspoon ground turmeric
- 1 teaspoon finely minced fresh ginger
- Pinch of ground red pepper
- 1 teaspoon pure maple syrup
- 2 tablespoons extra-virgin olive oil

Directions:

- ❖ Pour the quinoa and vegetable soup in a saucepan. Bring to a boil. Reduce the heat to low. Cover and cook for 15 minutes or until tender. Fluffy with a fork.
- ❖ Meanwhile, combine the ingredients for the mango sauce in a food processor. Pulse until smooth.
- ❖ Divide the quinoa, spinach, and cabbage into 4 serving bowls, then top with chickpeas, avocado, carrots, and bell pepper.
- ❖ Dress them with the mango sauce and spread with cilantro. Serve immediately.

39) Chili Bean Mix

Preparation Time: 15 minutes

Cooking Time: 5 hours

Servings: 4

Nutrition: Calories: 633 Fat: 16.3g Protein: 31.7g Carbs: 97.0g

Ingredients:

- 1 (28-ounce / 794-g) can chopped tomatoes, with the juice
- 1 (15-ounce / 425-g) can black beans, drained and rinsed
- 1 (15-ounce / 425-g) can redly beans, drained and rinsed
- 1 medium green bell pepper, chopped
- 1 yellow onion, chopped
- 1 tablespoon onion powder
- 1 teaspoon paprika
- 1 teaspoon cayenne pepper
- 1 teaspoon garlic powder
- ½ teaspoon ground black pepper
- 1 tablespoon olive oil
- 1 large hass avocado, pitted, peeled, and chopped, for garnish

Directions:

- ❖ Combine all the ingredients, except for the avocado, in the slow cooker. Stir to mix well.
- ❖ Put the slow cooker lid on and cook on high for 5 hours or until the vegetables are tender and the mixture has a thick consistency.
- ❖ Pour the chili in a large serving bowl. Allow to cool for 30 minutes, then spread with chopped avocado and serve.

40) Bean Balls with Red pepper and Marinara Sauce

Preparation Time: 15 minutes

Cooking Time: 30 minutes

Servings: 2-4

Nutrition: Calories: 351 Fat: 16.4g Protein: 11.5g Carbs: 42.9g

Ingredients:

Bean Balls:
- 1 tablespoon extra-virgin olive oil
- ½ yellow onion, minced
- 1 teaspoon fennel seeds
- 2 teaspoons dried oregano
- ½ teaspoon crushed red pepper flakes
- 1 teaspoon garlic powder
- 1 (15-ounce / 425-g) can white beans (cannellini or navy), drained and rinsed
- ½ cup whole-grain bread crumbs
- Ground black pepper, to taste

Marinara:
- 1 tablespoon extra-virgin olive oil
- 3 garlic cloves, minced
- Handful basil leaves
- 1 (28-ounce / 794-g) can chopped tomatoes with juice reserved

Directions:

❖ Preheat the oven to 350°F (180°C). Line a baking sheet with parchment paper. Heat the olive oil in a nonstick skillet over medium heat until shimmering.

❖ Add the onion and sauté for 5 minutes or until translucent. Sprinkle with fennel seeds, oregano, red pepper flakes, and garlic powder, then cook for 1 minute or until aromatic.

❖ Pour the sautéed mixture in a food processor and add the beans and bread crumbs. Sprinkle with ground black pepper, then pulse to combine well and the mixture holds together.

❖ Shape the mixture into balls with a 2-ounce (57-g) cookie scoop, then arrange the balls on the baking sheet.

❖ Bake in the preheated oven for 30 minutes or until lightly browned. Flip the balls halfway through the cooking time.

❖ While baking the bean balls, heat the olive oil in a saucepan over medium-high heat until shimmering. Add the garlic and basil and sauté for 2 minutes or until fragrant.

❖ Fold in the tomatoes and juice. Bring to a boil. Reduce the heat to low. Put the lid on and simmer for 15 minutes.

❖ Transfer the bean balls on a large plate and baste with marinara before serving.

DASH DIET

SIDE & SALAD

RECIPES

41) Veggie ChimiSalad

Preparation Time: 10 minutes

Cooking Time: 25 minutes

Servings: 4

Nutrition: Calories 231 Fat 20.1 g Carbs 20.1 g Protein 4.6 g

Ingredients:

- Roasted vegetables:
- 1 large sweet potato (chopped
- 6 red potatoes, quartered
- 2 whole carrots, chopped
- 2 tablespoons melted coconut oil
- 2 teaspoons curry powder
- 1 cup chopped broccolini
- 2 cups red cabbage, chopped
- 1 medium red bell pepper, sliced
- Chimichurri:
- 5 cloves garlic, chopped
- 1 medium serrano pepper
- 1 cup packed cilantro
- 1 cup parsley
- 3 tablespoons ripe avocado
- 3 tablespoons lime juice
- 1 tablespoon maple syrup
- Water to thin
- Salad:
- 4 cups hearty greens
- 1 medium ripe avocado, chopped
- 3 tablespoons hemp seeds
- Fresh herbs
- 5 medium radishes, sliced
- ¼ cup macadamia nut cheese

Directions:

- ❖ Preheat your oven to 400 degrees F.
- ❖ In a suitable bowl, toss all the vegetables for roasting with curry powder and oil.
- ❖ Divide these vegetables into two roasting pans.
- ❖ Bake the vegetables for 25 minutes in the oven.
- ❖ Meanwhile, in a blender, blend all chimichurri sauce ingredients until smooth.
- ❖ In a salad bowl, toss in all the roasted vegetables, chimichurri sauce and salad ingredients.
- ❖ Mix them well then refrigerate to chill.
- ❖ Serve.

42) Exotic Quinoa Bowl

Preparation Time: 15 minutes

Cooking Time: 15 minutes

Servings: 4

Nutrition: Calories: 669 Fat: 40g Protein: 17g Carbs: 69g

Ingredients:

- 1½ cups quinoa
- 2 cucumbers, seeded and diced
- 1 small red onion, diced
- 1 large tomato, diced
- 1 handful fresh flat-leaf parsley, chopped
- ½ cup extra-virgin olive oil
- ¼ cup red wine vinegar
- Juice of 1 lemon
- ¾ teaspoon freshly ground black pepper
- 4 heads endive, trimmed and separated into spears
- 1 avocado, pitted, peeled, and diced

Directions:

- ❖ In a saucepan, prepare the quinoa according to package directions. Rinse the quinoa under cold running water and drain very well. Transfer to a large bowl. Add the cucumbers, red onion, tomato, and parsley.
- ❖ In a small bowl, whisk together the olive oil, vinegar, lemon juice, and pepper. Pour the dressing over the quinoa mixture and toss to coat. Spoon the mixture onto the endive spears and top with the avocado.

43) Linguini with Peas and Parmigiano Reggiano

Preparation Time: 10 minutes

Cooking Time: 10 minutes

Servings: 4

Nutrition: Calories: 480 Protein: 20 g Fat: 11 g Carbs: 73 g

Ingredients:

- 2 eggs
- 1 cup frozen peas
- ½ cup Parmigiano-Reggiano cheese, grated
- 12 ounces linguini
- 1 Tbsp olive oil
- 1 onion, sliced
- Pepper, to taste

Directions:

- ❖ In a bowl, combine the zucchini noodles with pepper and the olive oil and toss well. Prepare linguini according to the package. Whisk eggs and mix in cheese.
- ❖ Sauté onion in olive oil, then stir in peas. Add pasta to pan. Add egg mixture to the pasta and cook for another 2 min. Season with pepper. Serve hot.

44) Noodles Salad with Peanut Butter Cream

Preparation Time: 10 minutes

Cooking Time: 0 minutes

Servings: 04

Nutrition: Calories 361 Fat 16.3 g Carbs 29.3 g Protein 3.3 g

Ingredients:
- Salad:
- 6 ounces vermicelli noodles, boiled
- 2 medium whole carrots, ribboned
- 2 stalks green onions, chopped
- ¼ cup cilantro, chopped
- 2 tablespoons mint, chopped
- 1 cup packed spinach, chopped
- 1 cup red cabbage, sliced
- 1 medium red bell pepper, sliced
- Dressing:
- ⅓ cup creamy peanut butter
- 3 tablespoons tamari
- 3 tablespoons maple syrup
- 1 teaspoon chili garlic sauce
- 1 medium lime, juiced
- ¼ cup water

Directions:
- ❖ Combine all the dressing ingredients in a small bowl.
- ❖ In a salad bowl, toss in the noodles, salad, and dressing.
- ❖ Mix them well then refrigerate to chill.
- ❖ Serve.

45) Delicious Potato Salad with Mustard

Preparation Time: 15 minutes

Cooking Time: 10 minutes

Servings: 4-6

Nutrition: Calories: 140 Carbs: 1g Fat: 15g Protein: 1g

Ingredients:
- ¼ cup extra-virgin olive oil
- ½ teaspoon pepper
- 1 garlic clove, peeled and threaded on skewer
- 1 small shallot, minced
- 1 tablespoon minced fresh chervil
- 1 tablespoon minced fresh chives
- 1 tablespoon minced fresh parsley
- 1 teaspoon minced fresh tarragon
- 1½ tablespoons white wine vinegar or Champagne vinegar
- 2 pounds small red potatoes, unpeeled, sliced ¼ inch thick
- 2 teaspoons Dijon mustard

Directions:
- ❖ Place potatoes in a big saucepan, put in water to cover by 1 inch, and bring to boil on high heat. Put in salt, decrease the heat to simmer, and cook until potatoes are soft and paring knife can be slipped in and out of potatoes with little resistance, about 6 minutes.
- ❖ While potatoes are cooking, lower skewered garlic into simmering water and blanch for 45 seconds. Run garlic under cold running water, then remove from skewer and mince.
- ❖ Reserve ¼ cup cooking water, then drain potatoes and lay out on tight one layer in rimmed baking sheet.
- ❖ Beat oil, minced garlic, vinegar, mustard, pepper, and reserved potato cooking water together in a container, then drizzle over potatoes. Let potatoes sit until flavors blend, about 10 minutes.
- ❖ Move potatoes to big container. Mix shallot and herbs in a small-sized container, then drizzle over potatoes and gently toss to coat using rubber spatula. Serve.

46) Easy Creamy Kernel

Preparation Time: 5minutes

Cooking Time:

Servings: 2

Nutrition: Carbs: 44.5g Protein: 11.5g Fats: 11.4g Calories: 306

Ingredients:
- Frozen peas: 1 cup can washed and drained
- Corn kernel: 2 cups can
- Sesame seeds: 2 tbsp
- Pepper: as per your taste
- Cashew cream: ½ cup

Directions:
- ❖ Combine all the ingredients
- ❖ Serve as the side dish

47) Green Bean with Walnut Mix

Preparation Time: 15 minutes

Cooking Time: 15 minutes

Servings: 6-8

Nutrition: Calories: 145 Carbs: 0g Fat: 8g Protein: 0g

Ingredients:

- ¼ cup walnuts
- ½ cup extra-virgin olive oil
- 1 scallion, sliced thin
- 2 garlic cloves, unpeeled
- 2 pounds green beans, trimmed
- 2½ cups fresh cilantro leaves and stems, tough stem ends trimmed (about 2 bunches)
- 4 teaspoons lemon juice

Directions:

- ❖ Cook walnuts and garlic in 8-inch frying pan on moderate heat, stirring frequently, until toasted and aromatic, 5 to 7 minutes; move to a container. Let garlic cool slightly, then peel and approximately chop.
- ❖ Process walnuts, garlic, cilantro, oil, lemon juice, scallion, and 1/8 teaspoon pepper using a food processor until smooth, about 1 minute, scraping down sides of the container as required; move to big container.
- ❖ Bring 4 quarts water to boil in large pot on high heat. In the meantime, fill big container halfway with ice and water.
- ❖ Put in green beans to boiling water and cook until crisp-tender, 3 to 5 minutes. Drain green beans, move to ice water, and allow to sit until chilled, approximately two minutes.
- ❖ Move green beans to a container with cilantro sauce and gently toss until coated. Sprinkle with pepper to taste. Serve.

48) Old School Panzanella

Preparation Time: 15 minutes

Cooking Time: 20 minutes

Servings: 6

Nutrition: Calories: 294 Carbs: 32g Fat: 15g Protein: 9g

Ingredients:

- 1 (15-ounce) can cannellini beans, rinsed
- 1 small red onion, halved and sliced thin
- 1½ pounds ripe tomatoes, cored and chopped, seeds and juice reserved
- 12 ounces rustic Italian bread, cut into 1-inch pieces (4 cups)
- 2 ounces Parmesan cheese, shaved
- 2 tablespoons minced fresh oregano
- 3 ounces (3 cups) baby arugula
- 3 tablespoons chopped fresh basil
- 3 tablespoons red wine vinegar
- 5 tablespoons extra-virgin olive oil

Directions:

- ❖ Place the oven rack in the center of the oven and pre-heat your oven to 350 degrees. Toss bread pieces with 1 tablespoon oil and sprinkle with pepper.
- ❖ Arrange bread in one layer in rimmed baking sheet and bake, stirring intermittently, until light golden brown, fifteen to twenty minutes. Allow it to cool to room temperature.
- ❖ Beat vinegar in a big container. Whisking continuously, slowly drizzle in remaining ¼ cup oil.
- ❖ Put in tomatoes with their seeds and juice, beans, onion, 1½ tablespoons basil, and 1 tablespoon oregano, toss to coat, and allow to sit for 20 minutes.
- ❖ Put in cooled croutons, arugula, remaining 1½ tablespoons basil, and remaining 1 tablespoon oregano and gently toss to combine.
- ❖ Sprinkle with pepper to taste. Move salad to serving platter and drizzle with Parmesan. Serve.

49) Vegan Chorizo Salad with Red Wine Vinegar

Preparation Time: 5 minutes

Cooking Time: 5 minutes

Servings: 4

Nutrition: Calories 138, Fat 8.95g, Carbs 5.63g, Protein 7.12g

Ingredients:

- 2 ½ tbsp olive oil
- 4 soy chorizo, chopped
- 2 tsp red wine vinegar
- 1 small red onion, finely chopped
- 2 ½ cups cherry tomatoes, halved
- 2 tbsp chopped cilantro
- Freshly ground black pepper to taste
- 3 tbsp sliced black olives to garnish

Directions:

- ❖ Over medium fire, heat half tablespoon of olive oil in a skillet and fry soy chorizo until golden. Turn heat off.
- ❖ In a salad bowl, whisk remaining olive oil and vinegar. Add onion, cilantro, tomatoes, and soy chorizo. Mix with dressing and season with black pepper.
- ❖ Garnish with olives and serve.

50) Juicy Smoked Apple Salad

Preparation Time: 15 minutes

Cooking Time: 0 minutes

Servings: 4-6

Nutrition: Calories: 157 Carbs: 12g Fat: 13g Protein: 1g

Ingredients:

- ¼ cup extra-virgin olive oil
- 1 fennel bulb, stalks discarded, bulb halved, cored, and sliced thin
- 1 small shallot, minced
- 1 tablespoon whole-grain mustard
- 2 Granny Smith apples, peeled, cored, and cut into 3-inch-long matchsticks
- 2 teaspoons minced fresh tarragon
- 3 tablespoons lemon juice
- 5 ounces (5 cups) watercress
- 6 ounces smoked mackerel, skin and pin bones removed, flaked
- Pepper

Directions:

- ❖ Beat lemon juice, mustard, shallot, 1 teaspoon tarragon, and ¼ teaspoon pepper together in a big container.
- ❖ Whisking continuously, slowly drizzle in oil. Put in watercress, apples, and fennel and gently toss to coat. Sprinkle with pepper to taste.
- ❖ Divide salad among plates and top with flaked mackerel. Sprinkle any remaining dressing over mackerel and drizzle with remaining 1 teaspoon tarragon. Serve instantly.

51) Kalamata Pepper Salad with Pine Nuts

Preparation Time: 10 minutes

Cooking Time: 20 minutes

Servings: 4

Nutrition: Calories 163, Fat 13.3g, Carbs 6.53g, Protein 3.37g

Ingredients:

- 8 large red bell peppers, deseeded and cut in wedges
- ½ tsp erythritol
- 2 ½ tbsp olive oil
- 1/3 cup arugula
- 1 tbsp mint leaves
- 1/3 cup pitted Kalamata olives
- 3 tbsp chopped almonds
- ½ tbsp balsamic vinegar
- Crumbled feta cheese for topping
- Toasted pine nuts for topping

Directions:

- ❖ Preheat oven to 400o F.
- ❖ Pour bell peppers on a roasting pan; season with erythritol and drizzle with half of olive oil. Roast in oven until slightly charred, 20 minutes. Remove from oven and set aside.
- ❖ Arrange arugula in a salad bowl, scatter bell peppers on top, mint leaves, olives, almonds, and drizzle with balsamic vinegar and remaining olive oil. Season with black pepper.
- ❖ Toss; top with feta cheese and pine nuts and serve.

52) Spiced Carrot Bowl

Preparation Time: 15 minutes

Cooking Time: 0 minutes

Servings: 4-6

Nutrition: Calories: 84 Carbs: 13g Fat: 4g Protein: 1g

Ingredients:

- 1/8 teaspoon cayenne pepper
- 1/8 teaspoon ground cinnamon
- ¾ teaspoon ground cumin
- 1-pound carrots, peeled and shredded
- 1 tablespoon lemon juice
- 1 teaspoon honey
- 2 oranges
- 3 tablespoons extra-virgin olive oil
- 3 tablespoons minced fresh cilantro

Directions:

- ❖ Cut away peel and pith from oranges. Holding fruit over bowl, use paring knife to slice between membranes to release segments.
- ❖ Cut segments in half crosswise and allow to drain in fine-mesh strainer set over big container, reserving juice.
- ❖ Beat lemon juice, honey, cumin, cayenne, cinnamon into reserved orange juice.
- ❖ Put in drained oranges and carrots and gently toss to coat. Allow to sit until liquid starts to pool in bottom of bowl, 3 to 5 minutes.
- ❖ Drain salad in fine-mesh strainer and return to now-empty bowl. Mix in cilantro and oil and sprinkle with pepper to taste. Serve.

53) Double Green Juicy Salad

Preparation Time: 10 minutes

Cooking Time: 15 minutes

Servings: 4

Nutrition: Calories 237, Fat 19.57g, Carbs 5.9g, Protein 12.75g

Ingredients:

- 1 (7 oz)block extra firm tofu
- 2 tbsp olive oil
- 2 tbsp butter
- 1 cup asparagus, trimmed and halved
- 1 cup green beans, trimmed
- 2 tbsp chopped dulse
- Freshly ground black pepper to taste
- ½ lemon, juiced
- 4 tbsp chopped walnuts

Directions:

- ❖ Place tofu in between two paper towels and allow soaking for 5 minutes. After, remove towels and chop into small cubes.
- ❖ Heat olive oil in a skillet and fry tofu until golden, 10 minutes. Remove onto a paper towel-lined plate and set aside.
- ❖ Melt butter in skillet and sauté asparagus
- ❖ And green beans until softened, 5 minutes. Add dulse, season with black pepper, and Cooking Time: until softened. Mix in tofu and stir-fry for 5 minutes.
- ❖ Plate, drizzle with lemon juice, and scatter walnuts on top.
- ❖ Serve warm.

54) *Lemony Orange Fennel Salad*

Preparation Time: 15 minutes

Cooking Time: 0 minutes

Servings: 4-6

Nutrition: Calories: 180 Carbs: 21g Fat: 11g Protein: 3g

Ingredients:

- ¼ cup coarsely chopped fresh mint
- ¼ cup extra-virgin olive oil
- ½ cup pitted oil-cured black olives, quartered
- 2 fennel bulbs, stalks discarded, bulbs halved, cored, and sliced thin
- 2 tablespoons lemon juice
- 4 blood oranges
- Pepper

Directions:

- ❖ Cut away peel and pith from oranges. Quarter oranges, then slice crosswise into ¼-inch-thick pieces. Mix oranges, fennel, olives, and mint in a big container.
- ❖ Beat lemon juice, and 1/8 teaspoon pepper together in a small-sized container. Whisking continuously, slowly drizzle in oil.
- ❖ Sprinkle dressing over salad and gently toss to coat. Sprinkle with pepper to taste. Serve.

55) *Asian Goji Salad*

Preparation Time: 10 minutes

Cooking Time: 2 minutes

Servings: 4

Nutrition: Calories 203, Fat 15.28g, Carbs 9.64g, Protein 6.67g, Protein 2.54g

Ingredients:

- 1 small head cauliflower, cut into florets
- 8 sun-dried tomatoes in olive oil, drained
- 12 pitted green olives, roughly chopped
- 1 lemon, zested and juiced
- 3 tbsp chopped green onions
- A handful chopped almonds
- ¼ cup goji berries
- 1 tbsp sesame oil
- ½ cup watercress
- 3 tbsp chopped parsley
- Freshly ground black pepper to taste
- Lemon wedges to garnish

Directions:

- ❖ Pour cauliflower into a large safe-microwave bowl, sprinkle with some water, and steam in microwave for 1 to 2 minutes or until softened.
- ❖ In a large salad bowl, combine cauliflower, tomatoes, olives, lemon zest and juice, green onions, almonds, goji berries, sesame oil, watercress, and parsley. Season with black pepper, and mix well.
- ❖ Serve with lemon wedges.

56) *Cheesy Asparagus Pesto Salad*

Preparation Time: 15 minutes

Cooking Time: 0 minutes

Servings: 4-6

Nutrition: Calories: 220 Carbs: 40g Fat: 5g Protein: 6g

Ingredients:

Pesto:

- ¼ cup fresh basil leaves
- ¼ cup grated Pecorino Romano cheese
- ½ cup extra-virgin olive oil
- 1 garlic clove, minced
- 1 teaspoon grated lemon zest plus 2 teaspoons juice
- 2 cups fresh mint leaves
- Pepper

Salad:

- ¾ cup hazelnuts, toasted, skinned, and chopped
- 2 oranges
- 2 pounds asparagus, trimmed
- 4 ounces feta cheese, crumbled (1 cup)
- Pepper

Directions:

- ❖ For the Pesto, process mint, basil, Pecorino, lemon zest and juice, garlic, and ¾ teaspoon salt using a food processor until finely chopped, approximately half a minute, scraping down sides of the container as required. Move to big container. Mix in oil and sprinkle with pepper to taste.
- ❖ For the Salad, chop asparagus tips from stalks into ¾-inch-long pieces. Cut asparagus stalks 1/8 inch thick on bias into approximate 2-inch lengths.
- ❖ Cut away the peel and pith from oranges. Holding fruit over bowl, use paring knife to cut between membranes to release segments.
- ❖ Put in asparagus tips and stalks, orange segments, feta, and hazelnuts to pesto and toss to combine. Sprinkle with pepper to taste. Serve.

57) *Ricotta Seed Salad*

Preparation Time: 15 minutes

Cooking Time:

Servings: 4

Nutrition: Calories 397, Fat 3.87g, Carbs 8.4g, Protein 8.93g

Ingredients:

- 2 tbsp olive oil
- 1 tbsp white wine vinegar
- 2 tbsp chia seeds
- Freshly ground black pepper to taste
- 2 cups broccoli slaw
- 1 cup chopped kelp, thoroughly washed and steamed
- 1/3 cup chopped pecans
- 1/3 cup pumpkin seeds
- 1/3 cup blueberries
- 2/3 cup ricotta cheese

Directions:

- ❖ In a small bowl, whisk olive oil, white wine vinegar, chia seeds, and black pepper. Set aside.
- ❖ In a large salad bowl, combine the broccoli slaw, kelp, pecans, pumpkin seeds, blueberries, and ricotta cheese.
- ❖ Drizzle dressing on top, toss, and serve.

58) Veggie Almond Chermoula Bowl

Preparation Time: 15 minutes

Cooking Time: 22 minutes

Servings: 4-6

Nutrition: Calories: 450 Carbs: 77g Fat: 7g Protein: 20g

Ingredients:

Salad:
- ½ cup raisins
- ½ red onion, sliced ¼ inch thick
- 1 cup shredded carrot
- 1 head cauliflower (2 pounds), cored and cut into 2-inch florets
- 2 tablespoons chopped fresh cilantro
- 2 tablespoons extra-virgin olive oil
- 2 tablespoons sliced almonds, toasted
- Pepper

Chermoula:
- 1/8 teaspoon cayenne pepper
- ¼ cup extra-virgin olive oil
- ½ teaspoon ground cumin
- ½ teaspoon paprika
- ¾ cup fresh cilantro leaves
- 2 tablespoons lemon juice
- 4 garlic cloves, minced

Directions:

❖ For the salad, place oven rack to lowest position and pre-heat your oven to 475 degrees. Toss cauliflower with oil and sprinkle with pepper.

❖ Arrange cauliflower in one layer in parchment paper–lined rimmed baking sheet. Cover tightly with aluminum foil and roast till they become tender, 5 to 7 minutes.

❖ Remove foil and spread onion evenly in sheet. Roast until vegetables are tender, cauliflower becomes deeply golden brown, and onion slices are charred at edges, 10 to 15 minutes, stirring halfway through roasting. Allow it to cool slightly, approximately five minutes.

❖ For the chermoula, process all ingredients using a food processor until smooth, about 1 minute, scraping down sides of the container as required. Move to big container.

❖ Gently toss cauliflower-onion mixture, carrot, raisins, and cilantro with chermoula until coated. Move to serving platter and drizzle with almonds. Serve warm or at room temperature.

59) Baked Asparagus Maple Salad

Preparation Time: 10 minutes

Cooking Time: 20 minutes

Servings: 4

Nutrition: Calories 146, Fat 12.87g, Carbs 5.07g, Protein 4.44g

Ingredients:
- 1 lb asparagus, trimmed and halved
- 2 tbsp olive oil
- ½ tsp dried basil
- ½ tsp dried oregano
- Freshly ground black pepper to taste
- ½ tsp hemp seeds
- 1 tbsp maple (sugar-freesyrup
- ½ cup arugula
- 4 tbsp crumbled feta cheese
- 2 tbsp hazelnuts
- 1 lemon, cut into wedges

Directions:

❖ Preheat oven to 350oF.

❖ Pour asparagus on a baking tray, drizzle with olive oil, basil, oregano, black pepper, and hemp seeds. Mix with your hands and roast in oven for 15 minutes.

❖ Remove, drizzle with maple syrup, and continue cooking until slightly charred, 5 minutes.

❖ Spread arugula in a salad bowl and top with asparagus. Scatter with feta cheese, hazelnuts, and serve with lemon wedges.

60) Cherry Kalamata Salad with Oregano

Preparation Time: 15 minutes

Cooking Time: 10 minutes

Servings: 4-6

Nutrition: Calories: 110 Carbs: 20g Fat: 4g Protein: 1g

Ingredients:
- ½ cup pitted kalamata olives, chopped
- ½ teaspoon sugar
- 1 shallot, minced
- 1 small cucumber, peeled, halved along the length, seeded, and cut into ½-inch pieces
- 1 tablespoon red wine vinegar
- 1½ pounds cherry tomatoes, quartered
- 2 garlic cloves, minced
- 2 tablespoons extra-virgin olive oil
- 2 teaspoons minced fresh oregano
- 3 tablespoons chopped fresh parsley
- 4 ounces feta cheese, crumbled (1 cup)
- Pepper

Directions:

❖ Toss tomatoes with sugar and ¼ teaspoon salt in a container and allow to sit for 30 minutes.

❖ Move tomatoes to salad spinner and spin until seeds and excess liquid have been removed, 45 to 60 seconds, stopping to redistribute tomatoes several times during spinning.

❖ Put in tomatoes, cucumber, olives, feta, and parsley to big container; set aside.

❖ Strain ½ cup tomato liquid through fine-mesh strainer into liquid measuring cup; discard remaining liquid.

❖ Bring tomato liquid, shallot, vinegar, garlic, and oregano to simmer in small saucepan on moderate heat and cook until reduced to 3 tablespoons, 6 to 8 minutes.

❖ Move to small-sized container and allow to cool to room temperature, approximately five minutes. Whisking continuously, slowly drizzle in oil.

❖ Sprinkle dressing over salad and gently toss to coat. Sprinkle with pepper to taste. Serve.

DASH DIET

MAIN RECIPES

7 courgette

61) Zucchini Rice with Chicken Chunks

Preparation Time: 10 minutes

Cooking Time: 14 minutes

Servings: 4

Nutrition: Calories 500 Fat 16.5 g Carbs 48 g Protein 38.7 g

Ingredients:

- 3 chicken breasts, skinless, boneless, and cut into chunks
- 1/4 fresh parsley, chopped
- 1 zucchini, sliced
- 2 bell peppers, chopped
- 1 cup rice, rinsed and drained
- 1 1/2 cup chicken broth
- 1 tbsp oregano
- 3 tbsp fresh lemon juice
- 1 tbsp garlic, minced
- 1 onion, diced
- 2 tbsp olive oil
- Pepper

Directions:

- ❖ Add oil into the inner pot of instant pot and set the pot on sauté mode. Add onion and chicken and cook for 5 minutes. Add rice, oregano, lemon juice, garlic, broth, pepper, and stir everything well.
- ❖ Seal pot with lid and cook on high for 4 minutes. Once done, release pressure using quick release. Remove lid. Add parsley, zucchini, and bell peppers and stir well.
- ❖ Seal pot again with lid and select manual and set timer for 5 minutes. Release pressure using quick release. Remove lid. Stir well and serve.

62) Smoked Baby Spinach Stew

Preparation Time: 10 minutes

Cooking Time: 25 minutes

Servings: 4

Nutrition: Calories 369 Fat 9.7g Carbs 67.9g Protein 18g

Ingredients:

- 1 splash olive oil
- 1 small onion, chopped
- 2 cloves garlic
- 5g cumin powder
- 5g smoked paprika
- ¼ teaspoon chili powder
- 235ml water
- 670g can diced tomatoes
- 165g cooked chickpeas (or can chickpeas
- 60g baby spinach
- A handful of chopped coriander, to garnish
- 20g slivered almonds, to garnish
- 4 slices toasted whole-grain bread, to serve

Directions:

- ❖ Heat olive oil in a saucepan over medium-high heat.
- ❖ Add onion and Cooking Time: until browned, for 7-8 minutes.
- ❖ Add garlic, cumin, paprika, and chili powder.
- ❖ Cooking Time: 1 minute.
- ❖ Add water and scrape any browned bits.
- ❖ Add the tomatoes and chickpeas. Season to taste and reduce heat.
- ❖ Simmer the soup for 10 minutes.
- ❖ Stir in spinach and Cooking Time: 2 minutes.
- ❖ Ladle soup in a bowl. Sprinkle with cilantro and almonds.
- ❖ Serve with toasted bread slices.

63) Green Chilis Chicken Breast

Preparation Time: 10 minutes

Cooking Time: 10 minutes

Servings: 3

Nutrition: Calories 237 Fat 8 g Carbs 10.8 g Protein 30.5 g

Ingredients:

- 2 chicken breasts, skinless and boneless
- 1 tbsp chili powder
- 1/2 tsp ground cumin
- 1/2 tsp garlic powder
- 1/4 tsp onion powder
- 1/2 tsp paprika
- 4 oz can green chilis, diced
- 1/4 cup chicken broth
- 14 oz can tomato, diced
- Pepper

Directions:

- ❖ Add all ingredients except chicken into the instant pot and stir well. Add chicken and stir. Seal pot with lid and cook on high for 10 minutes.
- ❖ Once done, allow to release pressure naturally for 5 minutes then release remaining using quick release. Remove lid.
- ❖ Remove chicken from pot and shred using a fork. Return shredded chicken to the pot and stir well. Serve and enjoy.

64) Chicken Breast with Italian Seasoning

Preparation Time: 10 minutes

Cooking Time: 12 minutes

Servings: 8

Nutrition: Calories 502 Fat 20 g Carbs 7.8 g Protein 66.8 g

Ingredients:

- 4 lb. chicken breasts, skinless and boneless
- 1 tbsp garlic powder
- 2 tbsp dried Italian herb mix
- 2 tbsp olive oil
- 1/4 cup chicken stock
- Pepper

Directions:

- ❖ Coat chicken with oil and season with dried herb, garlic powder, pepper. Place chicken into the instant pot. Pour stock over the chicken. Seal pot with a lid and select manual and set timer for 12 minutes.
- ❖ Once done, allow to release pressure naturally for 5 minutes then release remaining using quick release. Remove lid. Shred chicken using a fork and serve.

65) *Veggie Ragù Noodles*

Preparation Time: 10 minutes

Cooking Time: 15 minutes (plus 25 for lentils

Servings: 4

Nutrition: Calories 353 Fat 0.9g Carbs 74g Protein 17.7g

Ingredients:

- Bolognese:
- 100g red lentils
- 1 bay leaf
- Splash of olive oil
- 1 small onion, diced
- 1 large stalk celery, sliced
- 3 cloves garlic, minced
- 230ml tomato sauce or fresh pureed tomatoes
- 60ml red wine or vegetable stock (if you do not like wine
- 1 tablespoon fresh basil, chopped
- Pepper, to taste
- Soba noodles:
- 280g soba noodles

Directions:

- ❖ Cooking Time: the lentils; place lentils and bay leaf in a saucepan.
- ❖ Cover with water, so the water is 2-inches above the lentils.
- ❖ Bring to a boil over medium-high heat.
- ❖ Reduce heat and simmer the lentils for 25 minutes.
- ❖ Drain the lentils and discard the bay leaf.
- ❖ Heat a splash of olive oil in a saucepan.
- ❖ Add onion, and Cooking Time: 6 minutes.
- ❖ Add celery and Cooking Time: 2 minutes.
- ❖ Add garlic and Cooking Time: 2 minutes.
- ❖ Add the tomatoes and wine. Simmer the mixture for 5 minutes.
- ❖ Stir in the lentils and simmer 2 minutes.
- ❖ Remove the Bolognese from the heat and stir in basil.
- ❖ In the meantime, Cooking Time: the soba noodles according to package directions.
- ❖ Serve noodles with lentils Bolognese.

66) *Quinoa Chicken with Olives and Grrek Seasoning*

Preparation Time: 10 minutes

Cooking Time: 6 minutes

Servings: 4

Nutrition: Calories 566 Fat 16.4 g Carbs 57.4 g Protein 46.8 g

Ingredients:

- 1 lb. chicken breasts, skinless, boneless, and cut into chunks
- 14 oz can chickpeas, drained and rinsed
- 1 cup olives, pitted and sliced
- 1 cup cherry tomatoes, halved
- 1 cucumber, sliced
- 2 tsp Greek seasoning
- 1 1/2 cups chicken broth
- 1 cup quinoa, rinsed and drained
- Pepper

Directions:

- ❖ Add broth and quinoa into the instant pot and stir well. Season chicken with Greek seasoning, pepper and place into the instant pot.
- ❖ Seal pot with lid and cook on high for 6 minutes. Once done, release pressure using quick release. Remove lid. Stir quinoa and chicken mixture well.
- ❖ Add remaining ingredients and stir everything well. Serve immediately and enjoy it.

67) *Red Quinoa Burgers with Thaini Guacamole*

Preparation Time: 10 minutes

Cooking Time: 50 minutes

Servings: 4

Nutrition: Calories 343 Fat 16.6g Total Carbs 49.1g Protein 15g

Ingredients:

- Patties:
- 2 large beets, peeled, cubed
- 1 red onion, cut into chunks
- 115g red kidney beans
- 85g red cooked quinoa
- 2 cloves garlic, minced
- 30g almond meal
- 20g ground flax
- 10ml lemon juice
- ½ teaspoon ground cumin
- ½ teaspoon red pepper flakes
- 4 whole-meal burger buns
- Tahini Guacamole:
- 1 avocado, pitted, peeled
- 45ml lime juice
- 30g tahini sauce
- 5g chopped coriander

Directions:

- ❖ Preheat oven to 190C/375F.
- ❖ Toss beet and onion with a splash of olive oil.
- ❖ Bake the beets for 30 minutes.
- ❖ Transfer the beets and onion into a food blender.
- ❖ Add the beans and blend until coarse. You do not want a completely smooth mixture.
- ❖ Stir in quinoa, garlic, almond meal, flax seeds, lemon juice, cumin, and red pepper flakes.
- ❖ Shape the mixture into four patties.
- ❖ Transfer the patties to a baking sheet, lined with parchment paper.
- ❖ Bake the patties 20 minutes, flipping halfway through.
- ❖ In the meantime, make the tahini guac; mash the avocado with lime juice in a bowl.
- ❖ Stir in tahini and coriander. Season to taste.
- ❖ To serve; place the patty in the bun, top with guacamole and serve.

68) Rice and Beans with Red Bell pepper

Preparation Time: 10 minutes

Cooking Time: 1 hour 10 minutes

Servings: 6

Nutrition: Calories 469 Fat 6g Carbs 87.5g Protein 21.1g

Ingredients:

- 450g dry red kidney beans, soaked overnight
- 15ml olive oil
- 1 onion, diced
- 1 red bell pepper, seeded, diced
- 1 large stalk celery, sliced
- 4 cloves garlic, minced
- 15ml hot sauce
- 5g paprika
- 2g dried thyme
- 2 g parsley, chopped
- 2 bay leaves
- 900ml vegetable stock
- 280g brown rice
- Pepper, to taste

Directions:

- ❖ Drain the beans and place aside.
- ❖ Heat olive oil in a saucepot.
- ❖ Add onion and bell pepper. Cooking Time: 6 minutes.
- ❖ Add celery and Cooking Time: 3 minutes.
- ❖ Add garlic, hot sauce, paprika, and thyme. Cooking Time: 1 minute.
- ❖ Add the drained beans, bay leaves, and vegetable stock.
- ❖ Bring to a boil, and reduce heat.
- ❖ Simmer the beans for 1 hour 15 minutes or until tender.
- ❖ In the meantime, place rice in a small saucepot. Cover the rice with 4cm water.
- ❖ Season to taste and Cooking Time: the rice until tender, for 25 minutes.
- ❖ To serve; transfer ¼ of the beans into a food processor. Process until smooth.
- ❖ Combine the processed beans with the remaining beans and ladle into a bowl.
- ❖ Add rice and sprinkle with parsley before serving.

69) Baked Sole with Pistachos

Preparation Time: 5 minutes

Cooking Time: 10 minutes

Servings: 2

Nutrition: 166 Calories 6g Fat 2g Carbs 6g Protein

Ingredients:

- 4 (5 ounces) boneless sole fillets
- ½ cup pistachios, finely chopped
- Juice of 1 lemon
- teaspoon extra virgin olive oil

Directions:

- ❖ Pre-heat your oven to 350 degrees Fahrenheit
- ❖ Wrap baking sheet using parchment paper and keep it on the side
- ❖ Pat fish dry with kitchen towels and lightly season with salt and pepper
- ❖ Take a small bowl and stir in pistachios
- ❖ Place sol on the prepped sheet and press 2 tablespoons of pistachio mixture on top of each fillet
- ❖ Rub the fish with lemon juice and olive oil
- ❖ Bake for 10 minutes until the top is golden and fish flakes with a fork

70) Quinoa with Avocado and Pepper Mix

Preparation Time: 15 minutes

Cooking Time: 1 hour 5 minutes

Servings: 4

Nutrition: Calories 456 Total Fat 15.4g Carbs 71.1g Protein 8g

Ingredients:

- 160g quinoa
- 460ml vegetable stock
- 2 red bell peppers, cut in half, seeds and membrane removed
- 2 yellow bell peppers, cut in half, seeds, and membrane removed
- 120g salsa
- 15g nutritional yeast
- 10g chili powder
- 5g cumin powder
- 425g can black beans, rinsed, drained
- 160g fresh corn kernels
- Pepper, to taste
- 1 small avocado, sliced
- 15g chopped cilantro

Directions:

- ❖ Preheat oven to 190C/375F.
- ❖ Brush the baking sheet with some cooking oil.
- ❖ Combine quinoa and vegetable stock in a saucepan. Bring to a boil.
- ❖ Reduce heat and simmer 20 minutes.
- ❖ Transfer the quinoa to a large bowl.
- ❖ Stir in salsa, nutritional yeast, chili powder, cumin powder, black beans, and corn. Season to taste with pepper.
- ❖ Stuff the bell pepper halves with prepared mixture.
- ❖ Transfer the peppers onto a baking sheet, cover with aluminum foil, and bake for 30 minutes.
- ❖ Increase heat to 200C/400F and bake the peppers for an additional 15 minutes.
- ❖ Serve warm, topped with avocado slices, and chopped cilantro.

71) Lemony Mussels in Dry Wine Sauce

Preparation Time: 5 minutes

Cooking Time: 10 minutes

Servings: 2

Nutrition: Calories 22, 7 g fat, 1 g fiber, 18 g protein

Ingredients:

- 2 pounds small mussels
- 1 tablespoon extra-virgin olive oil
- 1 cup thinly sliced red onion
- 3 garlic cloves, sliced
- 1 cup dry white wine
- 2 (¼-inch-thick) lemon slices
- ¼ teaspoon freshly ground black pepper
- Fresh lemon wedges, for serving (optional)

Directions:

- ❖ In a large colander in the sink, run cold water over the mussels (but don't let the mussels sit in standing water).
- ❖ All the shells should be closed tight; discard any shells that are a little bit open or any shells that are cracked. Leave the mussels in the colander until you're ready to use them.
- ❖ In a large skillet over medium-high heat, heat the oil. Add the onion and cook for 4 minutes, stirring occasionally.
- ❖ Add the garlic and cook for 1 minute, stirring constantly. Add the wine, lemon slices, pepper, and bring to a simmer. Cook for 2 minutes.
- ❖ Add the mussels and cover. Cook for 3 minutes, or until the mussels open their shells. Gently shake the pan two or three times while they are cooking.
- ❖ All the shells should now be wide open. Using a slotted spoon, discard any mussels that are still closed. Spoon the opened mussels into a shallow serving bowl, and pour the broth over the top. Serve with additional fresh lemon slices, if desired.

72) Cold Spinach with Fruit Mix

Preparation Time: 5 minutes

Cooking Time: 0 minute

Servings: 1

Nutrition: Calories 296 Fat 18 g Carbs 27 g Protein 8 g

Ingredients:

- 3 cups baby spinach
- ½ cup strawberries, sliced
- 1 tablespoon white onion, chopped
- 2 tablespoons vinaigrette
- ¼ medium avocado, diced
- 2 tablespoons walnut, toasted

Directions:

- ❖ Put the spinach, strawberries and onion in a glass jar with lid.
- ❖ Drizzle dressing on top.
- ❖ Top with avocado and walnuts.
- ❖ Seal the lid and refrigerate until ready to serve.

73) Juiced Shrimp with Herbs

Preparation Time: 20 minutes

Cooking Time: 10 minutes

Servings: 2

Nutrition: Calories 190, 8 g fat, 1 g fiber, 24 g protein

Ingredients:

- 1 large orange
- 3 tablespoons extra-virgin olive oil, divided
- 1 tablespoon chopped fresh Rosemary
- 1 tablespoon chopped fresh thyme
- 3 garlic cloves, minced (about 1½ teaspoons)
- ¼ teaspoon freshly ground black pepper
- 1½ pounds fresh raw shrimp, shells, and tails removed

Directions:

- ❖ Zest the entire orange using a citrus grater. In a large zip-top plastic bag, combine the orange zest and 2 tablespoons of oil with the Rosemary, thyme, garlic and pepper
- ❖ Add the shrimp, seal the bag, and gently massage the shrimp until all the ingredients are combined and the shrimp is completely covered with the seasonings. Set aside.
- ❖ Heat a grill, grill pan, or a large skillet over medium heat. Brush on or swirl in the remaining 1 tablespoon of oil.
- ❖ Add half the shrimp, and cook for 4 to 6 minutes, or until the shrimp turn pink and white, flipping halfway through if on the grill or stirring every minute if in a pan. Transfer the shrimp to a large serving bowl.
- ❖ Repeat with the remaining shrimp, and add them to the bowl.
- ❖ While the shrimp cook, peel the orange and cut the flesh into bite-size pieces. Add to the serving bowl, and toss with the cooked shrimp. Serve immediately or refrigerate and serve cold.

74) Veggie Grill with Herbs and Cider Vinegar

Preparation Time: 15 minutes

Cooking Time: 6 minutes

Servings: 6

Nutrition: Calories 127 Fat 9 g Carbs 11 g Protein 3 g

Ingredients:
- 2 teaspoons cider vinegar
- 1 tablespoon olive oil
- ¼ teaspoon fresh thyme, chopped
- 1 teaspoon fresh parsley, chopped
- ¼ teaspoon fresh rosemary, chopped
- Pepper to taste
- 1 onion, sliced into wedges
- 2 red bell peppers, sliced
- 3 tomatoes, sliced in half
- 6 large mushrooms, stems removed
- 1 eggplant, sliced crosswise
- 3 tablespoons olive oil
- 1 tablespoon cider vinegar

Directions:
- ❖ Make the dressing by mixing the vinegar, oil, thyme, parsley, rosemary and pepper.
- ❖ In a bowl, mix the onion, red bell pepper, tomatoes, mushrooms and eggplant.
- ❖ Toss in remaining olive oil and cider vinegar.
- ❖ Grill over medium heat for 3 minutes.
- ❖ Turn the vegetables and grill for another 3 minutes.
- ❖ Arrange grilled vegetables in a food container.
- ❖ Drizzle with the herbed mixture when ready to serve.

75) Cheesy Gnocchi with Shrimp

Preparation Time: 10 minutes

Cooking Time: 20 minutes

Servings: 2

Nutrition: Calories 227, 7 g total fat, 1 g fiber, 20 g protein

Ingredients:
- 1 cup chopped fresh tomato
- 2 tablespoons extra-virgin olive oil
- 2 garlic cloves, minced
- ½ teaspoon freshly ground black pepper
- ¼ teaspoon crushed red pepper
- 1 (12-ounces) jar roasted red peppers
- 1-pound fresh raw shrimp, shells and tails removed
- 1-pound frozen gnocchi (not thawed)
- ½ cup cubed feta cheese
- 1/3 cup fresh torn basil leaves

Directions:
- ❖ Preheat the oven to 425°F. In a baking dish, mix the tomatoes, oil, garlic, black pepper, and crushed red pepper. Roast in the oven for 10 minutes.
- ❖ Stir in the roasted peppers and shrimp. Roast for 10 more minutes, until the shrimp turn pink and white.
- ❖ While the shrimp cooks, cook the gnocchi on the stovetop according to the package directions.
- ❖ Drain in a colander and keep warm. Remove the dish from the oven. Mix in the cooked gnocchi, feta, and basil, and serve.

76) Hummus Quinoa with Edamame Bowl

Preparation Time: 10 minutes

Cooking Time: 10 minutes

Servings: 4

Nutrition: Calories 381 Fat 19 g Carbs 43 g Protein 16 g

Ingredients:
- 8 oz. microwavable quinoa
- 2 tablespoons lemon juice
- ½ cup hummus
- Water
- 5 oz. baby kale
- 8 oz. cooked baby beets, sliced
- 1 cup frozen shelled edamame (thawed)
- ¼ cup sunflower seeds, toasted
- 1 avocado, sliced
- 1 cup pecans
- 2 tablespoons flaxseeds

Directions:
- ❖ Cooking Time: quinoa according to directions in the packaging.
- ❖ Set aside and let cool.
- ❖ In a bowl, mix the lemon juice and hummus.
- ❖ Add water to achieve desired consistency.
- ❖ Divide mixture into 4 condiment containers.
- ❖ Cover containers with lids and put in the refrigerator.
- ❖ Divide the baby kale into 4 food containers with lids.
- ❖ Top with quinoa, beets, edamame and sunflower seeds.
- ❖ Store in the refrigerator until ready to serve.
- ❖ Before serving add avocado slices and hummus dressing.

77) Fresh Salmon Fillet with Pepper

Preparation Time: 5 minutes

Cooking Time: 2 hours

Servings: 2

Nutrition: Calories 446, 20g fat, 65g protein

Ingredients:
- 2 (6-ounce / 170-g) salmon fillets
- 1 tablespoon olive oil
- 2 cloves garlic, minced
- ½ tablespoon lime juice
- 1 teaspoon finely chopped fresh parsley
- ¼ teaspoon black pepper

Directions:
- ❖ Spread a length of foil onto a work surface and place the salmon fillets in the middle.
- ❖ Blend olive oil, garlic, lime juice, parsley, and black pepper. Brush the mixture over the fillets. Fold the foil over and crimp the sides to make a packet.
- ❖ Place the packet into the slow cooker, cover, and cook on High for 2 hours
- ❖ Serve hot.

78) Delicious Puttanesca with Fresh Shrimp

Preparation Time: 5 minutes

Cooking Time: 15 minutes

Servings: 2

Nutrition: Calories 214, 10 g fat, 2 g fiber, 26 g protein

Ingredients:

- 2 tablespoons extra-virgin olive oil
- 3 anchovy fillets, drained and chopped
- 3 garlic cloves, minced
- ½ teaspoon crushed red pepper
- 1 (14.5-ounces) can low-sodium or no-salt-added diced tomatoes, undrained
- 1 (2.25-ounces) can sliced black olives, drained
- 2 tablespoons capers
- 1 tablespoon chopped fresh oregano
- 1-pound fresh raw shrimp, shells and tails removed

Directions:

- ❖ In a large skillet over medium heat, heat the oil. Mix in the anchovies, garlic, and crushed red pepper.
- ❖ Cook for 3 minutes, stirring frequently and mashing up the anchovies with a wooden spoon until they have melted into the oil.
- ❖ Stir in the tomatoes with their juices, olives, capers, and oregano. Turn up the heat to medium-high, and bring to a simmer.
- ❖ When the sauce is lightly bubbling, stir in the shrimp. Reduce the heat to medium, and cook the shrimp for 6 to 8 minutes, or until they turn pink and white, stirring occasionally, and serve.

79) Different Spicy Lasagna

Preparation Time: 15 minutes

Cooking Time: 40 minutes

Servings: 4

Nutrition: Calories: 194, Fat: 17.4g, Carbs:7g, Protein:7g

Ingredients:

- 2 tbsp butter
- 1 ½ lb ground tempeh
- Salt and ground black pepper to taste
- 1 tsp garlic powder
- 1 tsp onion powder
- 2 tbsp coconut flour
- 1 ½ cup grated mozzarella cheese
- 1/3 cup parmesan cheese
- 2 cups crumbled cottage cheese
- 1 large egg, beaten into a bowl
- 2 cups unsweetened marinara sauce
- 1 tbsp dried Italian mixed herbs
- ¼ tsp red chili flakes
- 4 large yellow squash, sliced
- ¼ cup fresh basil leaves

Directions:

- ❖ Preheat the oven to 375 F and grease a baking dish with cooking spray. Set aside.
- ❖ Melt the butter in a large skillet over medium heat and Cooking Time: the tempeh until brown, 10 minutes. Set aside to cool.
- ❖ In a medium bowl, mix the garlic powder, onion powder, coconut flour, black pepper, mozzarella cheese, half of the parmesan cheese, cottage cheese, and egg. Set aside.
- ❖ In another bowl, combine the marinara sauce, mixed herbs, and red chili flakes. Set aside.
- ❖ Make a single layer of the squash slices in the baking dish; spread a quarter of the egg mixture on top, a layer of the tempeh, then a quarter of the marinara sauce. Repeat the layering process in the same
- ❖ Ingredient proportions and sprinkle the top with the remaining parmesan cheese.
- ❖ Bake in the oven until golden brown on top, 30 minutes.
- ❖ Remove the dish from the oven, allow cooling for 5 minutes, garnish with the basil leaves, slice and serve.

80) Italian Green Seitan

Preparation Time: 15 minutes

Cooking Time: 18 minutes

Servings: 4

Nutrition: Calories: 582, Fat: 49.7g, Carbs:8g, Protein:31g,

Ingredients:

- 1 ½ lb seitan
- 3 tbsp almond flour
- Black pepper to taste
- 2 large zucchinis, cut into 2-inch slices
- 4 tbsp olive oil
- 2 tsp Italian mixed herb blend
- ½ cup vegetable broth

Directions:

- ❖ Preheat the oven to 400 F.
- ❖ Cut the seitan into strips and set aside.
- ❖ In a zipper bag, add the almond flour, salt, and black pepper. Mix and add the seitan slices. Seal the bag and shake to coat the seitan with the seasoning.
- ❖ Grease a baking sheet with cooking spray and arrange the zucchinis on the baking sheet. Season with black pepper, and drizzle with 2 tablespoons of olive oil.
- ❖ Using tongs, remove the seitan from the almond flour mixture, shake off the excess flour, and put two to three seitan strips on each zucchini.
- ❖ Season with the herb blend and drizzle again with olive oil.
- ❖ Cooking Time: in the oven for 8 minutes; remove the sheet and carefully pour in the vegetable broth. Bake further for 5 to 10 minutes or until the seitan cooks through.
- ❖ Remove from the oven and serve warm with low carb bread.

DASH DIET

SOUP RECIPES

81) Smoked Red Soup

Preparation Time: 10 minutes

Cooking Time: 17 minutes

Servings: 06

Nutrition: Calories 119 Fat 14 g Carbs 19 g Protein 5g

Ingredients:
- 1¼ cups red lentils, rinsed
- 4 cups of water
- ½ cup diced red bell pepper
- 1¼ cups red salsa
- 1 tablespoon chili powder
- 1 tablespoon dried oregano
- 1 teaspoon smoked paprika
- ¼ teaspoon black pepper
- ¾ cup frozen sweet corn
- 2 tablespoons lime juice

Directions:
- ❖ In a saucepan, add all the ingredients except the corn.
- ❖ Put on saucepan's lid and Cooking Time: for 15 minutes at a simmer.
- ❖ Stir in corn and Cooking Time: for another 2 minutes.
- ❖ Serve.

82) Lettuce Egg Soup Bowl

Preparation Time: 15 minutes

Cooking Time: 10 minutes

Servings: 2

Nutrition: Calories: 158 Carbs: 6.9g Fats: 7.3g Proteins: 15.4g

Ingredients:
- 32 oz vegetable broth
- 2 eggs
- 1 head romaine lettuce, chopped

Directions:
- ❖ Bring the vegetable broth to a boil and reduce the heat. Poach the eggs for 5 minutes in the broth and remove them into 2 bowls.
- ❖ Stir in romaine lettuce into the broth and cook for 4 minutes. Dish out in a bowl and serve hot.

83) Cayenne Kale and Mushrooms Soup

Preparation Time: 10 minutes

Cooking Time: 5 hrs. 5 minutes

Servings: 08

Nutrition: Calories 231 Fat 20.1 g Carbs 19,9 g Protein 4.6 g

Ingredients:
- ¼ cup olive oil
- 10 ounces button mushrooms, cleaned, and sliced
- 1½ teaspoons smoked paprika
- 1 pinch ground cayenne pepper
- 1 large onion, diced
- 2 cloves garlic, minced
- 2 pounds russet potatoes, peeled and diced
- 7 cups vegetable broth
- 8 ounces kale, sliced
- ½ teaspoon black pepper

Directions:
- ❖ In a pan, heat cooking oil and sauté mushrooms for 12 minutes.
- ❖ Season the mushrooms with salt, cayenne pepper, and paprika.
- ❖ Add olive oil and onion to a slow cooker.
- ❖ Sauté for 5 minutes then toss in rest of the soup ingredients.
- ❖ Put on the slow cooker's lid and Cooking Time: for 5 hours on low heat.
- ❖ Once done, puree the soup with a hand blender.
- ❖ Stir in sautéed mushrooms.
- ❖ Serve.

84) Coco Butternut Soup

Preparation Time: 15 minutes

Cooking Time: 1 hour & 35 minutes

Servings: 4

Nutrition: Calories: 149 Carbs: 6.6g Fats: 11.6g Proteins: 5.4g

Ingredients:
- 1 small onion, chopped
- 4 cups chicken broth
- 1 butternut squash
- 3 tablespoons coconut oil
- Nutmeg and pepper, to taste

Directions:
- ❖ Put oil and onions in a large pot and add onions. Sauté for about 3 minutes and add chicken broth and butternut squash.
- ❖ Simmer for about 1 hour on medium heat and transfer into an immersion blender. Pulse until smooth and season with pepper and nutmeg.
- ❖ Return to the pot and cook for about 30 minutes. Dish out and serve hot.

85) Cauliflower Broth with Leek

Preparation Time: 15 minutes

Cooking Time: 1 hour & 31 minutes

Servings: 4

Nutrition: Calories: 185 Carbs: 5.8g Fats: 12.7g Proteins: 10.8g

Ingredients:
- 4 cups chicken broth
- ½ cauliflower head, chopped
- 1 leek, chopped
- Black pepper, to taste

Directions:
- ❖ Put the cauliflower, leek and chicken broth into the pot and cook for about 1 hour on medium heat. Transfer into an immersion blender and pulse until smooth.
- ❖ Cook on for about 30 minutes on low heat. Season with pepper and serve.

86) Split Veggie Soup

Preparation Time: 10 minutes

Cooking Time: 6 hours

Servings: 12

Nutrition: Calories 361 Fat 16.3 g Carbs 29.3 g Protein 3.3 g

Ingredients:

- 1 cup dried, green split peas
- 2 cups celery, chopped
- 2 cups sliced carrots
- 1½ cups cauliflower, chopped
- 2 ounces dried shiitake mushrooms, chopped
- 9 ounces frozen artichoke hearts
- 11 cups water
- 1 teaspoon garlic powder
- 1½ teaspoon onion powder
- ½ teaspoon black pepper
- 1 tablespoon parsley
- ½ teaspoon ginger
- ½ teaspoon ground mustard seed
- ½ tablespoon brown rice vinegar

Directions:

- ❖ Add all the ingredients to a slow cooker.
- ❖ Put on the slow cooker's lid and Cooking
- ❖ Time: for 6 hours on low heat.
- ❖ Once done, garnish as desired.
- ❖ Serve warm.

87) Minestrone Bean Soup

Preparation Time: 10 minutes

Cooking Time: 2hrs 2 minutes

Servings: 4

Nutrition: Calories 205 Fat 19.7 g Carbs 26.1 g Protein 5.2 g

Ingredients:

- ½ sweet onion, chopped
- 4 garlic cloves, chopped
- 1 small head broccoli, chopped
- 2 stalks celery, chopped
- 1 cup green peas
- 3 green onions, chopped
- 2¾ cups vegetable broth
- 4 cups leafy greens
- 1 (15 ouncecan of cannellini beans
- Juice from 1 lemon
- 2 tablespoons fresh dill, chopped
- 5 fresh mint leaves
- ½ cup coconut milk
- Fresh herbs and peas, to garnish

Directions:

- ❖ In a slow cooker, add olive oil and onion.
- ❖ Sauté for 2 minutes then toss in the rest of the soup ingredients.
- ❖ Put on the slow cooker's lid and Cooking
- ❖ Time: for 2 hours on low heat.
- ❖ Once done, blend the soup with a hand blender.
- ❖ Garnish with fresh herbs and peas.
- ❖ Serve warm.

88) Swiss Coco Whisked Egg Soup

Preparation Time: 15 minutes

Cooking Time: 10 minutes

Servings: 4

Nutrition: Calories: 185 Carbs: 2.9g Fats: 11g Proteins: 18.3g

Ingredients:

- 3 cups bone broth
- 2 eggs, whisked
- 1 teaspoon ground oregano
- 3 tablespoons butter
- 2 cups Swiss chard, chopped
- 2 tablespoons coconut aminos
- 1 teaspoon ginger, grated
- Black pepper, to taste

Directions:

- ❖ Heat the bone broth in a saucepan and add whisked eggs while stirring slowly. Add the swiss chard, butter, coconut aminos, ginger, oregano and black pepper. Cook for about 10 minutes and serve hot.

89) Spinach and Mushroom Soup with Fresh Cream

Preparation Time: 15 minutes

Cooking Time: 10 minutes

Servings: 4

Nutrition: Calories: 160 Carbs: 7g Fats: 13.3g Proteins: 4.7g

Ingredients:

- 1 cup spinach, cleaned and chopped
- 100g mushrooms, chopped
- 1onion
- 6 garlic cloves
- ½ teaspoon red chili powder
- Black pepper, to taste
- 3 tablespoons buttermilk
- 1 teaspoon almond flour
- 2 cups chicken broth
- 3 tablespoons butter
- ¼ cup fresh cream for garnish

Directions:

- ❖ Heat butter in a pan and add onions and garlic. Sauté for about 3 minutes and add spinach and red chili powder.
- ❖ Sauté for about 4 minutes and add mushrooms. Transfer into a blender and blend to make a puree. Return to the pan and add buttermilk and almond flour for creamy texture.
- ❖ Mix well and simmer for about 2 minutes. Garnish with fresh cream and serve hot.

90) Veggie Soup with Peanut Butter

Preparation Time: 10 minutes

Cooking Time: 4 hrs. 5 minutes

Servings: 06

Nutrition: Calories 201 Fat 8.9 g Carbs 24.7 g Protein 15.3 g

Ingredients:

- 1 tablespoon water
- 6 cups sweet potatoes, peeled and chopped
- 2 cups onions, chopped
- 1 cup celery, chopped
- 4 large cloves garlic, chopped
- 2 teaspoons cumin seeds
- 3½ teaspoons ground coriander
- 1 teaspoon paprika
- ½ teaspoon crushed red pepper flakes
- 2 cups vegetable stock
- 3 cups water
- 4 tablespoons fresh ginger, grated
- 2 tablespoons natural peanut butter
- 2 cups cooked chickpeas
- 4 tablespoons lime juice
- Fresh cilantro, chopped
- Chopped peanuts, to garnish

Directions:

- ❖ In a slow cooker, add olive oil and onion.
- ❖ Sauté for 5 minutes then toss in the rest of the soup ingredients except chickpeas.
- ❖ Put on the slow cooker's lid and Cooking Time: for 4 hours on low heat.
- ❖ Once done, blend the soup with a hand blender.
- ❖ Stir in chickpeas and garnish with cilantro and peanuts.
- ❖ Serve warm.

91) Simple Red Lentil Soup

Preparation Time: 40 minutes

Cooking Time:

Servings: 3

Nutrition: Carbs: 15.3 g Protein: 6.2 g Fats: 0.3 g Calories: 90

Ingredients:

- Split red lentils: 1 cup
- Carrots: 1 cup grated
- Water: 6 cups
- Onion: 1 large coarsely chopped

Directions:

- ❖ Take a large saucepan and add water and bring to boil
- ❖ Add the chopped onions, carrots, lentils and bring to boil
- ❖ Lower the heat to medium and Cooking
- ❖ Time: for 20 minutes with partial cover
- ❖ Add the mixture to the high-speed blender to make a puree
- ❖ Whisk in water if desired
- ❖ Add again to the pan and slowly heat on a low flame for 10-15 minutes
- ❖ Add herbs or spices in between to augment the taste

92) Creamy Squash Soup

Preparation Time: 15 minutes

Cooking Time: 27 minutes

Servings: 5

Nutrition: Calories: 109 Carbs: 4.9g Fats: 8.5g Proteins: 3g

Ingredients:

- 1½ cups beef bone broth
- 1 small onion, peeled and grated.
- ¼ teaspoon poultry seasoning
- 2 small Delicata Squash, chopped
- 2 garlic cloves, minced
- 2 tablespoons olive oil
- ¼ teaspoon black pepper
- 1 small lemon, juiced
- 5 tablespoons sour cream

Directions:

- ❖ Put Delicata Squash and water in a medium pan and bring to a boil. Reduce the heat and cook for about 20 minutes. Drain and set aside.
- ❖ Put olive oil, onions, garlic and poultry seasoning in a small sauce pan. Cook for about 2 minutes and add broth. Allow it to simmer for 5 minutes and remove from heat.
- ❖ Whisk in the lemon juice and transfer the mixture in a blender. Pulse until smooth and top with sour cream.

93) Asparagus and Seed Soup with Cashew Cream

Preparation Time: 30 minutes

Cooking Time:

Servings: 2

Nutrition: Carbs: 11 g Protein: 9.4 g Fats: 18.3 g Calories: 243.5

Ingredients:

- Asparagus: 2 cups
- Vegetable stock: 4 cups
- Sesame seed: 2 tbsp
- Lemon juice: 1 tbsp
- Garlic: 4 cloves crushed
- Cashew cream: ½ cup
- Onion: 1 chopped
- Olive oil: 2 tbsp
- Pepper: as per your taste

Directions:

- ❖ Take a large saucepan and add olive oil to it
- ❖ Fry onion and garlic till it turns golden brown
- ❖ Chop asparagus and add to the pan along with the vegetable stock
- ❖ Let it boil and then Cooking Time: on low heat for 20 minutes
- ❖ When ready, add sesame seeds, lemon juice, and pepper as per your taste
- ❖ Serve with cashew cream on top

94) Spicy Bean Carrot and Lentil Soup

Preparation Time: 45 minutes

Cooking Time:

Servings: 4

Nutrition: Carbs: 425 g Protein: 8.17 g Fats: 4 g Calories: 148.75

Ingredients:

- Red lentils: 1 cup washed and drained
- Carrot: 2 medium chopped
- Beans: 1 cup drained
- Water: 3 cups
- Garlic: 3 cloves minced
- Onion: 1 medium finely chopped
- Ground cumin: 1 tsp
- Nutmeg: 1 tsp
- Ground coriander: 1 tsp
- Ground allspice: 1 tsp
- Ground cinnamon: 1 tsp
- Ground cayenne: ½ tsp
- Black pepper: as per your taste
- Extra virgin olive oil: 2 tbsp
- Cilantro: 1 tbsp chopped

Directions:

- ❖ Take a soup pot and heat oil in it on a medium flame
- ❖ Add onion and fry for 4-5 minutes
- ❖ Add carrot and garlic and stir for 5 minutes
- ❖ Wash lentils and add them to the pot
- ❖ Add water and bring to boil
- ❖ Lower the heat and Cooking Time: and cover for 15 minutes till lentil softens
- ❖ Add the remaining ingredients except for cilantro and Cooking Time: for an additional 15 minutes
- ❖ Serve warm with cilantro on top

95) Broccoli Ginger Soup with Herbs

Preparation Time: 15 minutes

Cooking Time: 37 minutes

Servings: 6

Nutrition: Calories: 183 Carbs: 5.2g Fats: 15.6g Proteins: 6.1g

Ingredients:

- 3 tablespoons ghee
- 5 garlic cloves
- 1 teaspoon sage
- ¼ teaspoon ginger
- 2 cups broccoli
- 1 small onion
- 1 teaspoon oregano
- ½ teaspoon parsley
- Black pepper, to taste
- 6 cups vegetable broth
- 4 tablespoons butter

Directions:

- ❖ Put ghee, onions, spices and garlic in a pot and cook for 3 minutes. Add broccoli and cook for about 4 minutes. Add vegetable broth, cover and allow it to simmer for about 30 minutes.
- ❖ Transfer into a blender and blend until smooth. Add the butter to give it a creamy delicious texture and flavor

96) Creamy Kabocha Soup

Preparation Time: 15 minutes

Cooking Time: 39 minutes

Servings: 8

Nutrition: Calories: 186 Carbs: 10.4g Fats: 14.9g Proteins: 3.7g

Ingredients:

- 1 apple, chopped
- 1 whole kabocha pumpkin, peeled, seeded and cubed
- 1 cup almond flour
- ¼ cup ghee
- 1 pinch cardamom powder
- 2 quarts water
- ¼ cup coconut cream
- 1 pinch ground black pepper

Directions:

- ❖ Heat ghee in the bottom of a heavy pot and add apples. Cook for about 5 minutes on a medium flame and add pumpkin.
- ❖ Sauté for about 3 minutes and add almond flour. Sauté for about 1 minute and add water. Lower the flame and cook for about 30 minutes.
- ❖ Transfer the soup into an immersion blender and blend until smooth. Top with coconut cream and serve.

97) Beans and Green Soup

Preparation Time: 20 minutes

Cooking Time:

Servings: 3

Nutrition: Carbs: 29.86 g Protein: 12.9 g Fats: 1.2 g Calories: 144

Ingredients:

- Cannellini beans: 1 cup rinsed and drained
- Artichoke hearts: 2 cups drained and chopped
- Frozen chopped spinach: 2 cups
- Water: 3 cups + 1 cup
- Garlic: 4 cloves chopped
- Onion: 1 medium chopped
- Italian herb blend: 2 tsp
- Black pepper: as per your taste

Directions:

- ❖ Take a blender and add onion, garlic, drained beans, herb blend, and pepper and add water
- ❖ Blend to give a smooth texture
- ❖ Add this puree to a large pan and Cooking Time: on medium-high heat
- ❖ When it initiates to boil, lower the heat and stir in between
- ❖ Let the mixture to thicken a bit
- ❖ Add one cup of water and spinach and blend
- ❖ Also, add artichokes and heat for 5 minutes
- ❖ Season with pepper if desired and serve

98) Sweety Onion Soup

Preparation Time: 15 minutes

Cooking Time: 335 minutes

Servings: 6

Nutrition: Calories: 198 Carbs: 6g Fats: 19.6g Proteins: 2.9g

Ingredients:

- 5 tablespoons butter
- 500 g brown onion medium
- 4 drops liquid stevia
- 4 tablespoons olive oil
- 3 cups beef stock

Directions:

- ❖ Put the butter and olive oil in a large pot over medium low heat and add onions. Cook for about 5 minutes and stir in stevia.
- ❖ Cook for another 5 minutes and add beef stock. Reduce the heat to low and simmer for about 25 minutes. Dish out into soup bowls and serve hot.

99) Lentils and Bean Mix in Masala Soup

Preparation Time: 40 minutes

Cooking Time:

Servings: 2

Nutrition: Carbs: 51.5 g Protein: 19.1 g Fats: 15.3 g Calories: 420

Ingredients:

- Red lentils: 1 cups
- Tomatoes: 1 cup can diced
- Beans: 1 cup can rinsed and drained
- Garam masala: 1 tbsp
- Vegetable oil: 2 tbsp
- Onion: 1 cup chopped
- Garlic: 3 cloves minced
- Ground cumin: 2 tbsp
- Smoked paprika: 1 tsp
- Celery: 1 cup chopped
- Lime juice and zest: 3 tbsp
- Fresh cilantro: 3 tbsp chopped
- Water: 2 cups

Directions:

- ❖ Take a large pot and add oil to it
- ❖ On the medium flame, add garlic, celery and onion
- ❖ Add garam masala, and cumin to them and stir for 5 minutes till they turn brown
- ❖ Add water, lentils, and tomatoes with the juice and bring to boil
- ❖ Bring to boil and heat for 25-30 minutes on low flame
- ❖ Add in lime juice and zest and beans of your choice and stir
- ❖ Serve with cilantro on top

100) Cauli Soup with Matcha Tea

Preparation Time: 15 minutes

Cooking Time: 13 minutes

Servings: 6

Nutrition: Calories: 79 Carbs: 3.8g Fats: 7.1g Proteins: 1.3g

Ingredients:

- 2 teaspoons thyme powder
- 1 head cauliflower
- 3 cups vegetable stock
- ½ teaspoon matcha green tea powder
- 3 tablespoons olive oil
- Black pepper, to taste
- 5 garlic cloves, chopped

Directions:

- ❖ Put the vegetable stock, thyme and matcha powder to a large pot over medium-high heat and bring to a boil. Add cauliflower and cook for about 10 minutes.
- ❖ Meanwhile, put the olive oil and garlic in a small sauce pan and cook for about 1 minute. Add the garlic and black pepper and cook for about 2 minutes.
- ❖ Transfer into an immersion blender and blend until smooth. Dish out and serve immediately.

DASH DIET
SNACK RECIPES

101) *Smoked Thaini Beets Hummus*

Preparation Time: 10 minutes

Cooking Time: 60 minutes

Servings: 4

Nutrition: Calories: 50.1 Cal Fat: 2.5 g Carbs: 5 g Protein: 2 g

Ingredients:

- 15 ounces cooked chickpeas
- 3 small beets
- 1 teaspoon minced garlic
- 1/2 teaspoon smoked paprika
- 1/4 teaspoon red chili flakes
- 2 tablespoons olive oil
- 1 lemon, juiced
- 2 tablespoon tahini
- 1 tablespoon chopped almonds
- 1 tablespoon chopped cilantro

Directions:

- ❖ Drizzle oil over beets, then wrap beets in a foil and bake for 60 minutes at 425 degrees F until tender.
- ❖ When done, let beet cool for 10 minutes, then peel and dice them and place them in a food processor.
- ❖ Add remaining ingredients and pulse for 2 minutes until smooth, tip the hummus in a bowl, drizzle with some more oil, and then serve straight away.

102) *Lemony Fava Cream*

Preparation Time: 10 minutes

Cooking Time: 30 minutes

Servings: 4

Nutrition: Calories 405 Fat 1 g Carbs 75 g Protein 25 g

Ingredients:

- 2 cups Santorini fava (yellow split peas), rinsed
- 2 medium onions, chopped
- 2 ½ cups water
- 2 cups +2 tablespoons vegetable broth
- To garnish:
- Lemon juice as required
- Chopped parsley

Directions:

- ❖ Place fava in a large pot. Add onions, broth, water and stir. Place over medium heat. When it begins to boil, reduce the heat and cook until fava is tender.
- ❖ Remove from heat and cool. Blend until creamy. Ladle into small plates. Add lemon juice and stir. Garnish with parsley and serve.

103) *Zucchini Hummus with Cumin*

Preparation Time: 5 minutes

Cooking Time: 0 minute

Servings: 8

Nutrition: Calories: 65 Cal Fat: 5 g Carbs: 3 g Protein: 2 g

Ingredients:

- 1 cup diced zucchini
- 1 teaspoon minced garlic
- 2 teaspoons ground cumin
- 3 tablespoons lemon juice
- 1/3 cup tahini

Directions:

- ❖ Place all the ingredients in a food processor and pulse for 2 minutes until smooth.
- ❖ Tip the hummus in a bowl, drizzle with oil and serve.

104) *Crispy Hummus Bell Pepper*

Preparation Time: 10 minutes

Cooking Time: 0 minutes

Servings: 2

Nutrition: Calories 136 Fat 7 g Carbs 13 g Protein 6 g

Ingredients:

- 4 tablespoons hummus
- 2 large whole grain crisp bread
- 4 tablespoons crumbled feta
- 1 small bell pepper, diced

Directions:

- ❖ Top the pieces of crisp bread with hummus. Sprinkle feta cheese and bell peppers and serve.

105) *Totopos Enchilados*

Preparation Time: 10 minutes

Cooking Time: 15 minutes

Servings: 4

Nutrition: Calories: 150 Fat: 7 g Carbs: 18 g Protein: 2 g

Ingredients:

- 12 ounces whole-wheat tortillas
- 4 tablespoons chipotle seasoning
- 1 tablespoon olive oil
- 4 limes, juiced

Directions:

- ❖ Whisk together oil and lime juice, brush it well on tortillas, then sprinkle with chipotle seasoning and bake for 15 minutes at 350 degrees F until crispy, turning halfway.
- ❖ When done, let the tortilla cool for 10 minutes, then break it into chips and serve.

106) Garlic Tomato Italian Toast

Preparation Time: 10 minutes

Cooking Time: 10 minutes

Servings: 3

Nutrition: Calories 162 Fat 4 g Carbs 29 g Protein 4 g

Ingredients:
- 3 tomatoes, finely chopped
- 1 clove garlic, minced
- ¼ teaspoon garlic powder (optional)
- A handful basil leaves, coarsely chopped
- Pepper to taste
- ½ teaspoon olive oil
- ½ tablespoon balsamic vinegar
- ½ tablespoon butter
- ½ baguette French bread or Italian bread, cut into ½ inch thick slices

Directions:
- ❖ Add tomatoes, garlic and basil in a bowl and toss well. Add pepper. Drizzle oil and vinegar and toss well. Set aside for an hour.
- ❖ Melt the butter and brush it over the baguette slices. Place in an oven and toast the slices. Sprinkle the tomato mixture on top and serve right away.

107) Spanish Potato Tortillas

Preparation Time: 10 minutes

Cooking Time: 8 minutes

Servings: 10

Nutrition: Calories: 70 Fat: 3 g Carbs: 8 g Protein: 1 g

Ingredients:
- 1/3 cup quinoa flour
- 1½ cups shredded sweet potato
- 1 cup grated carrot
- 1/3 teaspoon ground black pepper
- 2 teaspoons curry powder
- 2 flax eggs
- 2 tablespoons coconut oil

Directions:
- ❖ Place all the ingredients in a bowl, except for oil, stir well until combined and then shape the mixture into ten small patties
- ❖ Take a large pan, place it over medium-high heat, add oil and when it melts, add patties in it and Cooking Time: for 3 minutes per side until browned.
- ❖ Serve straight away

108) Turkish Delicious Spiced Falafel

Preparation Time: 30 minutes

Cooking Time: 15 minutes

Servings: 2

Nutrition: Calories 93 Fat 3.8 g Carbs 1.3 g Protein 3.9 g

Ingredients:
- 1 cup dried chickpeas (do not use cooked or canned)
- ½ cup fresh parsley leaves, discard stems
- ¼ cup fresh dill leaves, discard stems
- ½ cup fresh cilantro leaves
- 4 cloves garlic, peeled
- ½ tablespoon ground black pepper
- ½ tablespoon ground coriander
- ½ tablespoon ground cumin
- ½ teaspoon cayenne pepper (optional)
- ½ teaspoon baking powder
- ¼ teaspoon baking soda
- 1 tablespoon toasted sesame seeds
- Oil, as required

Directions:
- ❖ Rinse chickpeas and soak in water overnight. Cover with at least 3 inches of water. Drain and dry by patting with a kitchen towel.
- ❖ Add all the fresh herbs into a food processor. Process until finely chopped. Add chickpeas, spices and garlic and pulse for not more than 40 seconds each time until smooth.
- ❖ Transfer into a container. Cover and chill for at least 1 hour or until use. Divide the mixture into 12 equal portions and shape into patties.
- ❖ Place a deep pan over medium heat. Pour enough oil to cover at least 3 inches from the bottom of the pan.
- ❖ When the oil is well heated, but not smoking, drop falafel, a few at a time and fry until medium brown.
- ❖ Remove with a spoon and place on a plate lined with paper towels. Serve with a dip of your choice.

109) Red Pesto Bruschetta

Preparation Time: 5 minutes

Cooking Time: 0 minute

Servings: 4

Nutrition: Calories: 214 Fat: 7.2 g Carbs: 32 g Protein: 6.5 g

Ingredients:
- 1 small tomato, sliced
- ¼ teaspoon ground black pepper
- 1 tablespoon vegan pesto
- 2 tablespoons hummus
- 1 slice of whole-grain bread, toasted
- Hemp seeds as needed for garnishing

Directions:
- ❖ Spread hummus on one side of the toast, top with tomato slices and then drizzle with pesto.
- ❖ Sprinkle black pepper on the toast along with hemp seeds and then serve straight away.

110) *Cheesy Low-Fat Yogurt Dip*

Preparation Time: 15 minutes + chilling

Cooking Time: 0 minutes

Servings: 8 (2 tablespoons dip without vegetable sticks)

Nutrition: Calories 68 Fat 4 g Carbs 5 g Protein 4 g

Ingredients:
- 2 cups plain low-fat yogurt
- ¼ cup crumbled feta cheese
- 3 tablespoons chopped walnuts or pine nuts
- 1 teaspoon chopped fresh oregano or marjoram or ½ teaspoon dried oregano or marjoram, crushed
- Freshly ground pepper to taste
- 1 tablespoon snipped dried tomatoes (not oil packed)
- Walnut halves to garnish
- Assorted vegetable sticks to serve

Directions:
- ❖ For yogurt dip, place 3 layers of cotton cheesecloth over a strainer. Place strainer over a bowl. Add yogurt into the strainer. Cover the strainer with cling wrap. Refrigerate for 24-48 hours.
- ❖ Discard the strained liquid and add yogurt into a bowl. Add feta cheese, walnuts, seasoning, and herbs and mix well. Cover and chill for an hour.
- ❖ Garnish with walnut halves. Serve with vegetable sticks.

111) *Exotic Hummus And Sprout Toast*

Preparation Time: 5 minutes

Cooking Time: 0 minute

Servings: 4

Nutrition: Calories: 200 Fat: 10.5 g Carbs: 22 g Protein: 7 g

Ingredients:
- 1/2 of a medium avocado, sliced
- 1 slice of whole-grain bread, toasted
- 2 tablespoons sprouts
- 2 tablespoons hummus
- ¼ teaspoon lemon zest
- ½ teaspoon hemp seeds
- ¼ teaspoon red pepper flakes

Directions:
- ❖ Spread hummus on one side of the toast and then top with avocado slices and sprouts.
- ❖ Sprinkle with lemon zest, hemp seeds, and red pepper flakes and then serve straight away.

112) *Rich Ricotta Snack*

Preparation Time: 5 minutes

Cooking Time: 0 minutes

Servings: 2

Nutrition: Calories 178 Fat 9 g Carbs 15 g Protein 11 g

Ingredients:
- 2/3 cup part-skim ricotta
- 2 clementine's, peeled, separated into segments, deseeded
- 4 teaspoons chopped pistachio nuts

Directions:
- ❖ Place 1/3 cup ricotta in each of 2 bowls. Divide the clementine segments equally and place over the ricotta. Sprinkle pistachio nuts on top and serve.

113) *Sweety Apple Toast with Cinnamon*

Preparation Time: 5 minutes

Cooking Time: 0 minute

Servings: 4

Nutrition: Calories: 212 Fat: 7 g Carbs: 35 g Protein: 4 g

Ingredients:
- ½ of a small apple, cored, sliced
- 1 slice of whole-grain bread, toasted
- 1 tablespoon honey
- 2 tablespoons hummus
- 1/8 teaspoon cinnamon

Directions:
- ❖ Spread hummus on one side of the toast, top with apple slices and then drizzle with honey.
- ❖ Sprinkle cinnamon on it and then serve straight away.

114) *Crispy Zucchini*

Preparation Time: 10 minutes

Cooking Time: 120 minutes

Servings: 4

Nutrition: Calories: 54 Fat: 5 g Carbs: 1 g Protein: 6 g

Ingredients:
- 1 large zucchini, thinly sliced
- 2 tablespoons olive oil

Directions:
- ❖ Pat dry zucchini slices and then spread them in an even layer on a baking sheet lined with parchment sheet.
- ❖ Add oil, brush this mixture over zucchini slices on both sides and then bake for 2 hours or more until brown and crispy.
- ❖ When done, let the chips cool for 10 minutes and then serve straight away.

115) Summer Vegetarian Wraps

Preparation Time: 15 minutes

Cooking Time: 10 minutes

Servings: 2

Nutrition: Calories: 262; Fat: 15g; Carbs: 23g; Protein: 7g

Ingredients:

- 1½ cups seedless cucumber, peeled and chopped (about 1 large cucumber)
- 1 cup chopped tomato (about 1 large tomato)
- ½ cup finely chopped fresh mint
- 1 (2.25-ounce) can sliced black olives (about ½ cup), drained
- ¼ cup diced red onion (about ¼ onion)
- 2 tablespoons extra-virgin olive oil
- 1 tablespoon red wine vinegar
- ¼ teaspoon freshly ground black pepper
- ½ cup crumbled goat cheese (about 2 ounces)
- 4 whole-wheat flatbread wraps or soft whole-wheat tortillas

Directions:

- ❖ In a large bowl, mix together the cucumber, tomato, mint, olives, and onion until well combined.
- ❖ In a small bowl, whisk together the oil, vinegar, and pepper. Drizzle the dressing over the salad, and mix gently.
- ❖ With a knife, spread the goat cheese evenly over the four wraps. Spoon a quarter of the salad filling down the middle of each wrap.
- ❖ Fold up each wrap: Start by folding up the bottom, then fold one side over and fold the other side over the top. Repeat with the remaining wraps and serve.

116) Spiced Pineapple Mix

Preparation Time: 15 minutes

Cooking Time: 90 minutes

Servings: 4

Nutrition: Calories: 230 Fat: 17.5 g Carbs: 11.5 g Protein: 6.5 g

Ingredients:

- 5 cups mixed nuts
- 1 cup chopped dried pineapple
- 1 cup pumpkin seed
- 1 teaspoon garlic powder
- 1 teaspoon onion powder
- 2 teaspoons paprika
- 1/4 cup coconut sugar
- 1/2 teaspoon red chili powder
- 1/2 teaspoon ground black pepper
- 1 tablespoon red pepper flakes
- 1/2 tablespoon red curry powder
- 2 tablespoons soy sauce
- 2 tablespoons coconut oil

Directions:

- ❖ Switch on the slow cooker, add all the ingredients in it except for dried pineapple and red pepper flakes, stir until combined and Cooking Time: for 90 minutes at high heat setting, stirring every 30 minutes.
- ❖ When done, spread the nut mixture on a baking sheet lined with parchment paper and let it cool.
- ❖ Then spread dried pineapple on top, sprinkle with red pepper flakes and serve.

117) Salmon Wraps with Balsamic Vinegar

Preparation Time: 20 minutes

Cooking Time: 60 minutes

Servings: 2

Nutrition: Calories: 336; Total Fat: 16g; Carbs: 23g; Protein: 32g

Ingredients:

- 1-pound salmon filet, cooked and flaked, or 3 (5-ounce) cans salmon
- ½ cup diced carrots (about 1 carrot)
- ½ cup diced celery (about 1 celery stalk)
- 3 tablespoons chopped fresh dill
- 3 tablespoons diced red onion (a little less than 1/8 onion)
- 2 tablespoons capers
- 1½ tablespoons extra-virgin olive oil
- 1 tablespoon aged balsamic vinegar
- ½ teaspoon freshly ground black pepper
- 4 whole-wheat flatbread wraps or soft whole-wheat tortillas

Directions:

- ❖ In a large bowl, mix together the salmon, carrots, celery, dill, red onion, capers, oil, vinegar and pepper.
- ❖ Divide the salmon salad among the flatbreads. Fold up the bottom of the flatbread, then roll up the wrap and serve.

118) Incredible Dried Snack

Preparation Time: 10 minutes

Cooking Time: 17 minutes

Servings: 2

Nutrition: 44g Carbs, 7g Fat, 13g Protein, 285 Calories 65

Ingredients:

- 3 c. water
- ¼ c. cashew nut
- 8 dried apricots
- 4 dried figs
- 1 tsp. cinnamon

Directions:

- ❖ In a pot, mix water and quinoa and
- ❖ Let simmer for 15 minutes, until the water evaporates.
- ❖ Chop dried fruit.
- ❖ When quinoa is cooked, stir in all other ingredients.
- ❖ Serve cold. Add milk, if desired.

119) *Crispy Beet with Rosemary*

Preparation Time: 10 minutes

Cooking Time: 20 minutes

Servings: 3

Nutrition: Calories: 79 Fat: 4.7 g Carbs: 8.6 g Protein: 1.5 g

Ingredients:

- 3 large beets, scrubbed, thinly sliced
- 1/8 teaspoon ground black pepper
- 3 sprigs of rosemary, leaves chopped
- 4 tablespoons olive oil

Directions:

- Spread beet slices in a single layer between two large baking sheets, brush the slices with oil, then season with spices and rosemary, toss until well coated, and bake for 20 minutes at 375 degrees F until crispy, turning halfway.
- When done, let the chips cool for 10 minutes and then serve.

120) *Sweety Oats with Cinnamon*

Preparation Time: 10 minutes

Cooking Time: 15 minutes

Servings: 2

Nutrition: Calories: 232, Fat: 5.7 g, Carbs: 48.1 g, Protein: 5.2 g

Ingredients:

- ½ tsp. cinnamon
- ¼ tsp. ginger
- 2 apples make half-inch chunks
- ½ c. oats, steel cut
- 1½ c. water
- Maple syrup
- Clove
- ¼ tsp. nutmeg

Directions:

- Take Instant Pot and careful y arrange it over a clean, dry kitchen platform.
- Turn on the appliance.
- In the cooking pot area, add the water, oats, cinnamon, ginger, clove, nutmeg and apple. Stir the ingredients gently.
- Close the pot lid and seal the valve to avoid any leakage. Find and press the "Manual" cooking setting and set cooking time to 5 minutes.
- Allow the recipe ingredients to cook for the set time, and after that, the timer reads "zero."
- Press "Cancel" and press "NPR" setting for natural pressure release. It takes 8-10 times for all inside pressure to release.
- Open the pot and arrange the cooked recipe in serving plates.
- Sweeten as needed with maple or agave syrup and serve immediately.
- Top with some chopped nuts, optional.

DASH DIET

DESSERT

RECIPES

121) Cocoflakes Cantaloupe Yogurt with Raspberry

Preparation Time: 15 minutes

Cooking Time: 0 minutes

Servings: 6

Nutrition: Calories: 75 Fat: 4.1g Protein: 1.2g Carbs: 10.9g

Ingredients:

- 2 cups fresh raspberries, mashed
- 1 cup plain coconut yogurt
- ½ teaspoon vanilla extract
- 1 cantaloupe, peeled and sliced
- ½ cup toasted coconut flakes

Directions:

- ❖ Combine the mashed raspberries with yogurt and vanilla extract in a small bowl. Stir to mix well.
- ❖ Place the cantaloupe slices on a platter, then top with raspberry mixture and spread with toasted coconut. Serve immediately.

122) Plant-Based Berry and Banana Smoothie

Preparation Time: 5 minutes

Cooking Time:

Servings: 2

Nutrition: Calories 269, Fat 12.3g, Carbs 37.6g, Protein 6.4g

Ingredients:

- 2 cups, plant-based Milk
- 2 cups, Frozen or fresh berries
- ½ cup Frozen ripe bananas
- 2 teaspoons, Flax Seeds
- ¼ tsp, Vanilla
- ¼ tsp, Cinnamon

Directions:

- ❖ Mix together milk, flax seeds, and fruit. Blend in a high-power blender.
- ❖ Add cinnamon and vanilla. Blend until smooth.
- ❖ Serve and enjoy!

123) Delicious Apple Compote with Cinnamon

Preparation Time: 15 minutes

Cooking Time: 10 minutes

Servings: 4

Nutrition: Calories: 246 Fat: 0.9g Protein: 1.2g Carbs: 66.3g

Ingredients:

- 6 apples, peeled, cored, and chopped
- ¼ cup raw honey
- 1 teaspoon ground cinnamon
- ¼ cup apple juice

Directions:

- ❖ Put all the ingredients in a stockpot. Stir to mix well, then cook over medium-high heat for 10 minutes or until the apples are glazed by honey and lightly saucy. Stir constantly. Serve immediately.

124) Carrot and Prunes Smoothie with Walnuts

Preparation Time: 5 minutes

Cooking Time:

Servings: 4

Nutrition: Carbs: 14.9 g Protein: 3 g Fats: 4.5 g Calories: 103

Ingredients:

- Almond milk: 2 cups
- Prunes: 60 g
- Banana: 1
- Carrots: 150 g
- Walnuts: 30 g
- Ground cinnamon:½ tsp
- Vanilla extract:1 tsp

Directions:

- ❖ Add all the ingredients to the blender
- ❖ Blend on high speed to make it smooth

125) Choco Bombs

Preparation Time: 45 minutes

Cooking Time: 0 minutes

Servings: 15 balls

Nutrition: Calories: 146 Fat: 8.1g Protein: 4.2g Carbs: 16.9g

Ingredients:

- ¾ cup creamy peanut butter
- ¼ cup unsweetened cocoa powder
- 2 tablespoons softened almond butter
- ½ teaspoon vanilla extract
- 1¾ cups maple sugar

Directions:

- ❖ Line a baking sheet with parchment paper. Combine all the ingredients in a bowl. Stir to mix well.
- ❖ Divide the mixture into 15 parts and shape each part into a 1-inch ball. Arrange the balls on the baking sheet and refrigerate for at least 30 minutes, then serve chilled.

126) Dark Date and Banana Drink

Preparation Time: 5 minutes

Cooking Time:

Servings: 2

Nutrition: Carbs: 72.1 g Protein: 8 g Fats: 12.7 g Calories: 385

Ingredients:

- Unsweetened cocoa powder: 2 tbsp
- Unsweetened nut milk: 2 cups
- Almond butter: 2 tbsp
- Dried dates: 4 pitted
- Frozen bananas: 2 medium
- Ground cinnamon: ¼ tsp

Directions:

- ❖ Add all the ingredients to the blender
- ❖ Blend to form a smooth consistency

127) *Sweety Watermelon Iced Flakes*

Preparation Time: 10 minutes + 3 hours to freeze

Cooking Time: 0 minutes

Servings: 4

Nutrition: Calories: 153 Carbs: 39g Protein: 2g Fat: 1g

Ingredients:

• 4 cups watermelon cubes
• ¼ cup honey
• ¼ cup freshly squeezed lemon juice

Directions:

❖ In a blender, combine the watermelon, honey, and lemon juice. Purée all the ingredients, then pour into a 9-by-9-by-2-inch baking pan and place in the freezer.

❖ Every 30 to 60 minutes, run a fork across the frozen surface to fluff and create ice flakes. Freeze for about 3 hours total and serve.

128) *Cashew and Fruit Mix Smoothie*

Preparation Time: 5 minutes

Cooking Time:

Servings: 4

Nutrition: Carbs: 32.9 g Protein: 9.7 g Fats: 15 g Calories: 320

Ingredients:

• Pistachios: 1 cup
• Raw pumpkin:175 g
• Cloves:1
• Nutmeg:1/8 tsp
• Dates: 4
• Banana:1
• Ground ginger:1/8 tsp
• Ground cinnamon:1 tsp
• Cashew milk:500 ml
• Ice: as per your need

Directions:

❖ Add all the ingredients to the blender
❖ Blend on high speed to make it smooth

129) *Seed Butter Cookies*

Preparation Time: 10 minutes

Cooking Time: 15 minutes

Servings: 14-16

Nutrition: Calories 218 Fat 12g Carbs 25g Protein 4g

Ingredients:

• 1 cup sesame seeds, hulled
• 1 cup sugar
• 8 tablespoons unsalted butter, softened
• 2 large eggs
• 1¼ cups flour

Directions:

❖ Preheat the oven to 350°F. Toast the sesame seeds on a baking sheet for 3 minutes. Set aside and let cool.

❖ Using a mixer, cream together the sugar and butter. Put the eggs one at a time until well-blended. Add the flour and toasted sesame seeds and mix until well-blended.

❖ Drop spoonful of cookie dough onto a baking sheet and form them into round balls, about 1-inch in diameter, similar to a walnut.

❖ Put in the oven and bake for 5 to 7 minutes or until golden brown. Let the cookies cool and enjoy.

130) *Persimmon Healthy Smoothie*

Preparation Time: 5 minutes

Cooking Time:

Servings: 1

Nutrition: Carbs: 37.1 g Protein: 6.5 g Fats: 5.4 g Calories: 183

Ingredients:

• Persimmon: 1
• Spinach: 1 cup
• Orange: 1
• Water: 1 cup
• Chia seeds:1 tbsp

Directions:

❖ Add all the ingredients to the blender
❖ Blend to form a smooth consistency
❖ Add ice cubes from the top to chill it

131) *Sweety Rice with Rose Water and Dried Figs*

Preparation Time: 45 minutes

Cooking Time: 0 minutes

Servings: 2

Nutrition: Calories: 228; Fat: 6.1g; Carbs: 35.1g; Protein: 7.1g

Ingredients:

• 3 cups milk
• 1 cup water
• 2 tablespoons sugar
• 1/3 cup white rice, rinsed
• 1 tablespoon honey
• 4 dried figs, chopped
• 1/2 teaspoon cinnamon
• 1/2 teaspoon rose water

Directions:

❖ In a deep saucepan, bring the milk, water and sugar to a boil until the sugar has dissolved.

❖ Stir in the rice, honey, figs, raisins, cinnamon, and turn the heat to a simmer; let it simmer for about 40 minutes, stirring periodically to prevent your pudding from sticking.

❖ Afterwards, stir in the rose water. Divide the pudding between individual bowls and serve. Bon appétit!

132) Fresh and Dry Smoothie

Preparation Time: 5 minutes

Cooking Time:

Servings: 1

Nutrition: Carbs: 66.0 g Protein: 16.1 g Fats: 18 g Calories: 435

Ingredients:
- Fresh figs: 2
- Almond milk: 1 cup
- Dried date: 1 pitted
- Vanilla extract: ¼ tsp
- Sesame seeds: 2 tbsp

Directions:
- ❖ Add all the ingredients to the blender
- ❖ Blend to form a smooth consistency

133) Greek Yogurt with Honey and Fruit Mix

Preparation Time: 10 minutes

Cooking Time: 0 minutes

Servings: 2

Nutrition: Calories: 98; Fat: 0.2g; Carbs: 20.7g; Protein: 2.8g

Ingredients:
- 8 clementine orange segments
- 8 medium-sized strawberries
- 8 pineapple cubes
- 8 seedless grapes
- 1/2 cup Greek-style yogurt
- 1/2 teaspoon vanilla extract
- 2 tablespoons honey

Directions:
- ❖ Thread the fruits onto 4 skewers.
- ❖ In a mixing dish, thoroughly combine the yogurt, vanilla, and honey.
- ❖ Serve alongside your fruit kabobs for dipping. Bon appétit!

134) Almond Berries and Banana Smoothie

Preparation Time: 5 minutes

Cooking Time:

Servings: 2

Nutrition: Carbs: 14.9 g Protein: 2.2 g Fats: 1.6 g Calories: 92

Ingredients:
- Banana: 1 ripe
- Frozen berries: 200g
- Almond milk: 250ml

Directions:
- ❖ Add all the ingredients in the blender
- ❖ Blend to give a smooth consistency
- ❖ Pour to the glasses and serve

135) Choco Walnuts Cube with Thaini

Preparation Time: 10 minutes

Cooking Time: 0 minutes

Servings: 2

Nutrition: Calories: 198; Fat: 13g; Carbs: 17.3g; Protein: 4.6g

Ingredients:
- 8 ounces bittersweet chocolate
- 1 cup tahini paste
- 1/4 cup almonds, chopped
- 1/4 cup walnuts, chopped

Directions:
- ❖ Microwave the chocolate for about 30 seconds or until melted. Stir in the tahini, almonds, and walnuts.
- ❖ Spread the batter into a parchment-lined baking pan. Place in your refrigerator until set, for about 3 hours.
- ❖ Cut into cubes and serve well-chilled.

136) Fruit Explosion Smoothie

Preparation Time: 5 minutes

Cooking Time:

Servings: 2

Nutrition: Carbs: 52.8 g Protein: 6.4 g Fats: 19.5 g Calories: 407

Ingredients:
- Banana: 1 ripe sliced
- Almond milk: 1 cup
- Coconut oil: 1 tbsp
- Powdered ginger: 1 tsp
- Frozen fruit medley: 1 cup
- Chia seeds: 2 tbsp

Directions:
- ❖ Add all the ingredients in the blender
- ❖ Blend to give a smooth consistency
- ❖ Pour to the glasses and serve

137) Greek Granola Berries

Preparation Time: 10 minutes

Cooking Time: 0 minutes

Servings: 2

Nutrition: Calories: 238; Fat: 16.7g; Carbs: 53g; Protein: 21.6g

Ingredients:
- 2 cups Greek yogurt
- 2 cups mixed berries
- 1/2 cup granola

Directions:
- ❖ Alternate layers of mixed berries, granola, and yogurt until two dessert bowls are filled completely.
- ❖ Cover and place in your refrigerator until you're ready to serve. Bon appétit!

138) *Energy Almond Smoothie*

Preparation Time: 5 minutes

Cooking Time:

Servings: 1

Nutrition: Carbs: 41.2 g Protein: 8.9 g Fats: 3.9 g Calories: 220

Ingredients:

- Large banana: 1 frozen
- Fresh spinach: 1 cup
- Rolled oats: 2 tbsp
- Unsweetened almond milk: ¾ cup

Directions:

- ❖ Add all the ingredients to the blender
- ❖ Blend to form a smooth consistency

139) *Figs and Walnuts with Honey Topping*

Preparation Time: 20 Minutes

Cooking Time: 0 Minutes

Servings: 4

Nutrition: Calories: 110 Carbs: 26 Fat: 3g, Protein: 1g

Ingredients:

- 12 dried figs
- 2 Tbsps. thyme honey
- 2 Tbsps. sesame seeds
- 24 walnut halves

Directions:

- ❖ Cut off the tough stalk ends of the figs.
- ❖ Slice open each fig.
- ❖ Stuff the fig openings with two walnut halves and close
- ❖ Arrange the figs on a plate, drizzle with honey, and sprinkle the sesame seeds on it.
- ❖ Serve.

140) *Thaini Figs Smoothie*

Preparation Time: 5 minutes

Cooking Time:

Servings: 1

Nutrition: Carbs: 66.0 g

Protein: 12.1 g Fats: 16.5g Calories: 435

Ingredients:

- Dried date: 1 pitted
- Tahini: 1 tbsp
- Fresh figs: 2
- Almond milk: 1 cup
- Vanilla extract: ¼ tsp

Directions:

- ❖ Add all the ingredients to the blender
- ❖ Blend to form a smooth consistency

Chapter 9 - Simple Dr. Cole's Meal Plan – For Women

Day 1

3) Golden Coco Mix | Calories 259

21) Pasta with Delicious Spanish Salsa | Calories 364

62) Smoked Baby Spinach Stew | Calories 369

41) Veggie ChimiSalad | Calories 231

123) Delicious Apple Compote with Cinnamon | Calories 246

Total Calories: 1469

Day 2

10) Black Olives and Feta Bread | Calories 251

25) Chickpeas Tomato Pasta with Tamari | Calories 442

65) Veggie Ragù Noodles | Calories 353

46) Easy Creamy Kernel | Calories 306

125) Choco Bombs | Calories 146

Total Calories: 1498

Day 3

13) Vegetables Wraps with Soy Sauce | Calories 284

29) Spiced Kidney Pasta with Cilantro | Calories 274

67) Red Quinoa Burgers with Thaini Guacamole | Calories 343

48) Old School Panzanella | Calories 294

128) Cashew and Fruit Mix Smoothie | Calories 320

Total Calories: 1515

Day 4

19) Awesome Breakfast Muesli | Calories 250

31 Red Lentils Spaghetti with Herbs | Calories 335

72) Cold Spinach with Fruit Mix | Calories 296

53) Double Green Juicy Salad | Calories 237

140) Thaini Figs Smoothie | Calories 435

Total Calories: 1553

Day 5

7) Button Mushroom Omelette | Calories 189

35) Macaroni with Cherry and Peas | Calories 320

76) Hummus Quinoa with Edamame Bowl | Calories 381

56) Cheesy Asparagus Pesto Salad | Calories 220

138) Energy Almond Smoothie | Calories 220

Total Calories: 1330

Day 6

4) Delicious Agave Rice | Calories 192

37) Golden Rice with Pistachios | Calories 320

75) Cheesy Gnocchi with Shrimp | Calories 227

55) Asian Goji Salad | Calories 203

136) Fruit Explosion Smoothie | Calories 407

Total Calories: 1349

Day 7

2) Apple Warm Oatmeal | Calories 200

40) Bean Balls with Red pepper and Marinara Sauce | Calories 351

63) Green Chilis Chicken Breast | Calories 237

44) Noodles Salad with Peanut Butter Cream | Calories 361

126) Dark Date and Banana Drink | Calories 385

Total Calories: 1534

DASH
Diet Cookbook
For Athlete

Dr. Cole's Full Energy Meal Plan | Delicious Low Sodium Recipes For Women and Men to Increase your Performance with No Stress Diet

By Janeth Cole

Chapter 1 -   Introduction

Everyone knows that in order to have a fit body, physical exercise and a proper diet is essential, besides it is the right way to take care of your health. The DASH Diet gives athletes the option of consuming a variety of foods, eliminating those that add too many calories and too few nutrients.

If you do sports and want to lose weight or stay at your ideal weight, controlling your diet is essential to achieve your goals. The DASH diet works because it is a plan that is low in saturated fat, cholesterol and sodium. In fact, Harvard University recommends the DASH diet as a way to eat healthy, balanced meals.

What is the DASH diet?

The DASH diet (Dietary Approaches to Stop Hypertension) emerged in 1997, it is based on a balanced consumption of the different main nutrients and stands out for its low sodium content.

With the DASH diet you will increase the consumption of fruits, vegetables, whole grains, fish, lean meat, seeds, foods rich in potassium, calcium and magnesium, and for frying or seasoning you can use olive, coconut or soybean oil. Fatty foods, sugary foods, soft drinks and alcohol, as well as processed products should be avoided, reduced or eliminated from your daily diet.

Benefits of DASH diet for athletes

The diet is not restrictive and you can adapt it to the type of sport you do. For example, if you practice aerobic activities, you should control the intake of sufficient slow-absorption carbohydrates. By taking the right amount, you will have the energy you need to avoid becoming overweight.

The most important thing with DASH Dieti is that it avoids excess salt, which is responsible for fluid retention. If you do sports and reduce your intake, you will notice that your body increases its diuretic function, helping you to eliminate toxins and fats. The Dash diet limits carbohydrate-rich foods, reducing the number of calories and totally eliminates sutured and trans fats along with sugars and refined flours. Therefore, it is ideal to lose weight while practicing sports and a good way to improve your diet as an athlete on a daily basis.

Other benefits are: it avoids arterial hypertension, prevents type II diabetes, improves cholesterol levels, takes care of your heart preventing cardiovascular diseases, protects your bones from osteoporosis.

DASH DIET
BREAKFAST

1) *Maple Quinoa Porridge*

Preparation Time: 5 minutes

Cooking Time: 35 minutes

Servings: 2

Nutrition: Calories 474 Fat 13.3g Carbs 73.2g Protein 17.8g

Ingredients:
- 85g quinoa
- 70g amaranth
- 460ml water
- 115ml unsweetened soy milk
- ½ teaspoon vanilla paste
- 15g almond butter
- 30ml pure maple syrup
- 10g raw pumpkin seeds
- 10g pomegranate seeds

Directions:
- ❖ Combine quinoa, amaranth, and water.
- ❖ Bring to a boil over medium-high heat.
- ❖ Reduce heat and simmer the grains, stirring occasionally, for 20 minutes.
- ❖ Stir in milk and maple syrup.
- ❖ Simmer for 6-7 minutes. Remove from the heat and stir in vanilla, and almond butter.
- ❖ Allow the mixture to stand for 5 minutes.
- ❖ Divide the porridge between two bowls.
- ❖ Top with pumpkin seeds and pomegranate seeds.
- ❖ Serve.

2) *Chickpea Multigrain Toast*

Preparation Time: 10 minutes

Cooking Time: 15 minutes

Servings: 4

Nutrition: Calories: 337 Carbs: 43g Fat: 13g Protein: 13g

Ingredients:
- 15 oz. can Chickpeas
- 2 oz. - ½ cup Diced feta cheese
- 1 Pitted avocado
- Fresh juice:
- 2 tsp. Lemon (or 1 tbsp. orange)
- ½ tsp. Black pepper
- 2 tsp. Honey
- 4 slices Multigrain toast

Directions:
- ❖ Toast the bread. Drain the chickpeas in a colander. Scoop the avocado flesh into the bowl. Use a large fork/potato masher to mash them until the mix is spreadable.
- ❖ Pour in the lemon juice, pepper, and feta. Combine and divide onto the four slices of toast. Drizzle using the honey and serve

3) *Festival Portobello Crepes*

Preparation Time: 20 minutes + inactive time

Cooking Time: 15 minutes

Servings: 4

Nutrition: Calories 428 Fat 13.3g Carbs 60.3g Protein 22.6g

Ingredients:

Crepes:
- 140g chickpea flour
- 30g peanut flour
- 5g nutritional yeast
- 5g curry powder
- 350ml water

Filling:
- 10ml olive oil
- 4 portabella mushroom caps, thinly sliced
- 1 onion, thinly sliced
- 30g baby spinach

Vegan mayo:
- 60ml aquafaba
- 1/8 teaspoon cream of tartar
- ¼ teaspoon dry mustard powder
- 15ml lemon juice
- 5ml raw cider vinegar
- 15ml maple syrup
- 170ml avocado oil

Directions:
- ❖ Make the mayo; combine aquafaba, cream of tartar, mustard powder. Lemon juice, cider vinegar, and maple syrup in a bowl.
- ❖ Beat with a hand mixer for 30 seconds.
- ❖ Set the mixer to the highest speed. Drizzle in avocado oil and beat for 10 minutes or until you have a mixture that resembles mayonnaise.
- ❖ Of you want paler (in the color mayo add more lemon juice.
- ❖ Refrigerate for 1 hour.
- ❖ Make the crepes; combine chickpea flour, peanut flour, nutritional yeast, curry powder and water in a food blender.
- ❖ Blend until smooth.
- ❖ Heat large non-stick skillet over medium-high heat. Spray the skillet with some cooking oil.
- ❖ Pour ¼ cup of the batter into skillet and with a swirl motion distribute batter all over the skillet bottom.
- ❖ Cooking Time: the crepe for 1 minute per side. Slide the crepe onto a plate and keep warm.
- ❖ Make the filling; heat olive oil in a skillet over medium-high heat.
- ❖ Add mushrooms and onion and Cooking Time: for 6-8 minutes.
- ❖ Add spinach and toss until wilted, for 1 minute.
- ❖ Transfer into a large bowl.
- ❖ Fold in prepared vegan mayo.
- ❖ Spread the prepared mixture over chickpea crepes. Fold gently and serve.

4) _Taste Almond Bagel_

Preparation Time: 5 minutes

Cooking Time: 8 minutes

Servings: 4

Nutrition: Calories: 187 Protein: 7 g Fat: 9 g Carbs: 18 g

Ingredients:

- 1/2 cup Fisher Sliced Almonds
- 1 cup whole milk ricotta
- 1/4 teaspoon almond extract
- zest from an orange, optional
- 1 teaspoon honey
- hearty whole-grain toast
- English muffin or bagel
- extra Fisher sliced almonds
- sliced peaches
- extra honey for drizzling

Directions:

- ❖ Cut peaches into a proper shape and then brush them with olive oil. After that, set it aside. Take a bowl; combine the ingredients for the filling. Set aside.
- ❖ Then just pre-heat grill to medium. Place peaches cut side down onto the greased grill. Close lid cover and then just grill until the peaches have softened, approximately 6-10 minutes, depending on the size of the peaches.
- ❖ Then you will have to place peach halves onto a serving plate. Put a spoon of about 1 tablespoon of ricotta mixture into the cavity (you are also allowed to use a small scooper).
- ❖ Sprinkle it with slivered almonds, crushed amaretti cookies, and honey. Decorate with the mint leaves

5) _Grains Breakfast_

Preparation Time: 10 minutes

Cooking Time:

Servings: 2

Nutrition: Calories 339 Fat 14.3g Carbs 41.8g Protein 13.1g

Ingredients:

- 15g chia seeds
- 10g buckwheat
- 15g hemp seeds
- 20g Goji berries
- 235mml vanilla soy milk

Directions:

- ❖ Combine chia, buckwheat, hemp seeds, and Goji berries in a bowl.
- ❖ Heat soy milk in a saucepan until start to simmer.
- ❖ Pour the milk over "cereals".
- ❖ Allow the cereals to stand for 5 minutes.
- ❖ Serve.

6) _Eggs Tarte with Spinach & Feta_

Preparation Time: 10 minutes

Cooking Time: 20 minutes

Servings: 8

Nutrition: Calories: 240 Protein: 9 g Fat: 16 g Carbs: 13 g

Ingredients:

- 1 cup spinach, finely diced
- 1/2 yellow onion, finely diced
- 1/2 cup sliced sun-dried tomatoes
- 4 large basil leaves, finely diced
- 1/3 cup feta cheese crumbles
- 8 large eggs
- 1/4 cup milk (any kind)

Directions:

- ❖ Warm the oven to 375°F. Then, roll the dough sheet into a 12x8-inch rectangle. Then, cut in half lengthwise.
- ❖ After that, you will have to cut each half crosswise into 4 pieces, forming 8 (4x3-inch) pieces dough. Then, press each into the bottom and up sides of the ungreased muffin cup.
- ❖ Trim dough to keep the dough from touching, if essential. Set aside. Then, you will have to combine the eggs, salt, pepper in the bowl and beat it with a whisk until well mixed. Set aside.
- ❖ Melt the butter in 12-inch skillet over medium heat until sizzling; add bell peppers. You will have to cook it, stirring occasionally, 2-3 minutes or until crisply tender.
- ❖ After that, add spinach leaves; continue cooking until spinach is wilted. Then just add egg mixture and prosciutto.
- ❖ Divide the mixture evenly among prepared muffin cups. Finally, bake it for 14-17 minutes or until the crust is golden brown

7) _Monkey Cream_

Preparation Time: 10 minutes

Cooking Time:

Servings: 2

Nutrition: Calories 272, Fat 14.3g, Carbs 37g, Protein 6.2g,

Ingredients:

- 2 frozen ripe bananas, chopped
- 1/3 cup frozen strawberries
- 2 tbsp cocoa powder
- 2 tbsp salted almond butter
- 2 cups unsweetened vanilla almond milk
- 1 dash Stevia or agave nectar
- 1/3 cup ice

Directions:

- ❖ Add all ingredients in a blender and blend until smooth.
- ❖ Take out and serve.

8) Greek Pancakes

Preparation Time: 10 minutes

Cooking Time: 5 minutes

Servings: 2

Nutrition: Calories: 166 Protein: 14 g Fat: 5 g Carbs: 52g

Ingredients:

- 1 cup all-purpose flour
- 1 cup whole-wheat flour
- 4 teaspoons baking powder
- 1 tablespoon sugar
- 1 1/2 cups unsweetened almond milk
- 2 teaspoons vanilla extract
- 2 large eggs
- 1/2 cup plain 2% Greek yogurt
- Fruit, for serving
- Maple syrup, for serving

Directions:

- ❖ First, you will have to pour the curds into the bowl and mix them well until creamy. After that, you will have to add egg whites and mix them well until combined.
- ❖ Then take a separate bowl, pour the wet mixture into the dry mixture. Stir to combine. The batter will be extremely thick.
- ❖ Then, simply spoon the batter onto the sprayed pan heated too medium-high. The batter must make 4 large pancakes.
- ❖ Then, you will have to flip the pancakes once when they start to bubble a bit on the surface. Cook until golden brown on both sides

9) Fast Strawberries Breakfast Bowl

Preparation Time: 5 minutes

Cooking Time: 10 minutes

Servings: 2

Nutrition: calories 200, fat 5g, carbs 25g, protein 8.6g

Ingredients:

- 1/3 cup old-fashioned rolled oats
- 2 tablespoon dried strawberries
- 2 cups water
- 2/3 cup almond milk
- ½ teaspoon coconut sugar

Direction:

- ❖ Put the water in your instant pot.
- ❖ Add strawberries, oats, almond milk and sugar.
- ❖ Cooking Time: on High for 10 minutes, leave aside to release pressure, transfer the oats to breakfast bowls and serve.
- ❖ Enjoy!

10) Spinach Muffins

Preparation Time: 15 minutes

Cooking Time: 15 minutes

Servings: 12

Nutrition: Calories: 113 Protein: 6 g Fat: 7 g Carbs: 5 g

Ingredients:

- 2 cups baby spinach finely chopped
- 1 cup chopped or sliced cherry tomatoes
- 1/2 cup finely chopped onion
- 1 tablespoon chopped fresh oregano
- 1 cup crumbled feta cheese
- 1/2 cup chopped \'7bpitted\'7d kalamata olives
- 2 teaspoons high oleic sunflower oil
- 1 cup cooked quinoa
- 8 eggs

Directions:

- ❖ Pre-heat oven to 350 degrees Fahrenheit, and then prepare 12 silicone muffin holders on the baking sheet, or just grease a 12-cup muffin tin with oil and set aside.
- ❖ Finely chop the vegetables and then heat the skillet to medium. After that, add the vegetable oil and onions and sauté for 2 minutes.
- ❖ Then, add tomatoes and sauté for another minute, then add spinach and sauté until wilted, about 1 minute.
- ❖ Place the beaten egg into a bowl and then add lots of vegetables like feta cheese, quinoa, veggie mixture and then stir well until everything is properly combined.
- ❖ Pour the ready mixture into greased muffin tins or silicone cups, dividing the mixture equally. Then, bake it in an oven for 30 minutes or so.

11) Quinoa Breakfast Bowl

Preparation Time: 10 minutes

Cooking Time: 3 minutes

Servings: 6

Nutrition: 120, fat 10, carbs 12, protein 5

Ingredients:

- 1 and ½ cups quinoa
- 2 tablespoons maple syrup
- 2 and ¼ cups water
- ¼ teaspoon cinnamon, ground
- ½ teaspoon vanilla
- Sliced almond for serving

Direction:

- ❖ In your instant pot, mix water with maple syrup, quinoa, cinnamon and vanilla.
- ❖ Cooking Time: on high pressure for 1 minute, leave 10 minutes aside to release pressure, pour into breakfast bowls and serve with sliced almond on top.
- ❖ Enjoy!

12) Date & Bannana Under Zero

Preparation Time: 5 minutes

Cooking Time: 20 minutes

Servings: 2

Nutrition: Calories: 350 Protein: 14 g Fat: 12 g Carbs: 49 g

Ingredients:

- ¼ Cup Greek Yogurt, Plain
- 1/3 cup of yogurt
- 2/3 cup of oats
- 1 cup of milk
- 2 tsp date syrup or you can also use maple syrup or honey
- 1 mashed banana
- ¼ tsp cinnamon
- ¼ cup walnuts

Directions:

- ❖ Firstly, get a mason jar or a small bowl and add all the ingredients. After that stir and mix all the ingredients well. Cover it securely, and cool it in a refrigerator overnight.
- ❖ After that, take it out the next morning, add more liquid or cinnamon if required, and serve cold. (However, you can also microwave it for people with a warmer palate.)

13) Oatmeal Taste Cinnamon

Preparation Time: 10 minutes

Cooking Time: 4 minutes

Servings: 6

Nutrition: calories 130, fat 3g, carbs 12g, protein 4g

Ingredients:

- 1 and ½ cups steel cut oats
- 1 and ½ cups pumpkin puree
- 4 and ½ cups water
- 1 teaspoon allspice
- 1 teaspoon vanilla
- 2 teaspoons cinnamon powder
- ½ cup coconut sugar
- ¼ cup pecans, chopped
- 1 tablespoon cinnamon
- Almond milk for serving

Direction:

- ❖ Put the water in your instant pot.
- ❖ Add oats, pumpkin puree, 2 teaspoons cinnamon, vanilla and allspice.
- ❖ Stir, cover, Cooking Time: on High for 3 minutes and then release pressure.
- ❖ Meanwhile, in a bowl, mix pecans with sugar and 1 tablespoon cinnamon and stir well.
- ❖ Sprinkle this over pumpkin oatmeal and serve with almond milk.
- ❖ Enjoy!

14) Tomato, Seeded and Chopped Salad

Preparation Time: 20 minutes

Cooking Time: 15 minutes

Servings: 8

Nutrition: Calories: 99 Fat: 7g Carbs: 7g Protein: 3.4g

Ingredients:

- 1 large eggplant, washed and cubed
- 1 tomato, seeded and chopped
- 1 small onion, diced
- 2 tablespoons parsley, chopped
- 2 tablespoons extra virgin olive oil
- 2 tablespoons distilled white vinegar
- ½ cup feta cheese, crumbled

Directions:

- ❖ Pre-heat your outdoor grill to medium-high. Pierce the eggplant a few times using a knife/fork. Cook the eggplants on your grill for about 15 minutes until they are charred.
- ❖ Keep it on the side and allow them to cool. Remove the skin from the eggplant and dice the pulp. Transfer the pulp to a mixing bowl and add parsley, onion, tomato, olive oil, feta cheese and vinegar.
- ❖ Mix well and chill for 1 hour. Enjoy!

15) Cashews Breakfast

Preparation Time: 10 minutes

Cooking Time: 35 minutes

Servings: 6

Nutrition: calories 70, fat 1g, carbs 5g, protein 1g

Ingredients:

- ¼ cup split yellow gram, roasted
- 1 tablespoon split Bengal gram, roasted
- 1 and ½ cups banana, chopped
- 1 cup almond milk
- 1 cup rice, washed
- 3 cups water
- 2 cups jaggery, chopped
- 3 tablespoons cashews, chopped
- 1 teaspoon cardamom powder
- 2 tablespoons raisins
- ¼ teaspoon nutmeg powder
- Some saffron strands

Directions:

- ❖ In your instant pot, mix yellow and Bengal gram with rice, almond milk and 2 and ½ cups water and Cooking Time: on High for 5-6 minutes.
- ❖ Release pressure and leave aside for now.
- ❖ In a bowl, mix jaggery with the rest of the water, stir and pour everything into a pan heated over medium high heat.
- ❖ Cooking Time: for 7 minutes, stirring often and then add the rice and gram mix.
- ❖ Stir again and Cooking Time: for 4 minutes.
- ❖ Add raisins, cashews, stir and Cooking Time: for 2 minutes.
- ❖ Add cardamom powder, nutmeg powder, saffron and bananas, stir and Cooking Time: for 1 minute.
- ❖ Pour this into breakfast bowls and serve right away.
- ❖ Enjoy!

16) Asiago Frittata

Preparation Time: 5 minutes

Cooking Time: 10 minutes

Servings: 4

Nutrition: Calories: 199 Fat: 13g Carbs: 5g Protein: 16g

Ingredients:

- 8 large eggs
- ¼ cup Asiago cheese, grated
- 1 tablespoon fresh basil, chopped
- 1 teaspoon fresh oregano, chopped
- 1 teaspoon extra virgin olive oil
- 1 teaspoon garlic, minced
- 1 cup canned artichokes, drained
- 1 tomato, chopped

Directions:

- ❖ Pre-heat your oven to broil. Take a medium bowl and whisk in eggs, Asiago cheese, oregano, basil and pepper. Blend in a bowl.
- ❖ Place a large ovenproof skillet over medium-high heat and add olive oil. Add garlic and sauté for 1 minute. Remove skillet from heat and pour in egg mix.
- ❖ Return skillet to heat and sprinkle artichoke hearts and tomato over eggs. Cook frittata without stirring for 8 minutes.
- ❖ Place skillet under the broiler for 1 minute until the top is lightly browned. Cut frittata into 4 pieces and serve. Enjoy!

17) Tapioca Pudding

Preparation Time: 10 minutes

Cooking Time: 8 minutes

Servings: 6

Nutrition: calories 180, fat 2.5g, carbs 39g, protein 2.5g

Ingredients:

- 1/3 cup tapioca pearls, washed and drained
- ½ cup water
- ½ cup coconut sugar
- 1 and ¼ cups almond milk
- Zest from ½ lemon

Directions:

- ❖ Put the tapioca pearls in a bowl and mix with water, sugar, milk and lemon zest.
- ❖ Stir well, transfer this to your instant pot and Cooking Time: on High for 8 minutes.
- ❖ Release pressure, leave the pudding aside for 10 minutes, pour it into breakfast bowls and serve right away!
- ❖ Enjoy!

18) Fresh Eggs

Preparation Time: 15 minutes

Cooking Time: 20 minutes

Servings: 5

Nutrition: Calories: 198 Fat: 12g Carbs: 17g Protein: 8g

Ingredients:

- 2 acorn squash
- 6 whole eggs
- 2 tablespoons extra virgin olive oil
- 5-6 pitted dates
- 8 walnut halves
- A fresh bunch of parsley

Directions:

- ❖ Pre-heat your oven to 375 degrees Fahrenheit. Slice squash crosswise and prepare 3 slices with holes. While slicing the squash, make sure that each slice has a measurement of ¾ inch thickness.
- ❖ Remove the seeds from the slices. Take a baking sheet and line it with parchment paper. Transfer the slices to your baking sheet and season them with pepper.
- ❖ Bake in your oven for 20 minutes. Chop the walnuts and dates on your cutting board. Take the baking dish out of the oven and drizzle slices with olive oil.
- ❖ Crack an egg into each of the holes in the slices and season with pepper. Sprinkle the chopped walnuts on top. Bake for 10 minutes more. Garnish with parsley and add maple syrup

19) Veggie Breakfast

Preparation Time: 10 minutes

Cooking Time: 20 minutes

Servings: 4

Nutrition: calories 179, fat 2g, carbs 18g, protein 7g

Ingredients:

- 1 yellow onion, chopped
- 3 tablespoons olive oil
- 1 carrot, chopped
- 2 cups mushrooms, sliced
- Zest from ½ lemon, grated
- 2 tablespoons lemon juice
- 4 garlic cloves, minced
- 1 cup quinoa
- 10 cherry tomatoes, halved
- 1 cup veggie stock
- 1 tablespoon spring onions, chopped

Directions:

- ❖ Set your instant pot on sauté mode, add oil, heat it up, add onion and carrot, stir and sauté for 2 minutes.
- ❖ Add mushrooms, stir and Cooking Time: for 3 minutes more.
- ❖ Add pepper, garlic, lemon juice and lemon zest, quinoa and stock, stir and Cooking Time: for 1 minute.
- ❖ Add tomatoes, cover pot, Cooking Time: on High for 10 minutes, divide into bowls, sprinkle spring onion on top and serve cold for breakfast.
- ❖ Enjoy!

20)Blueberries & Barley Bowl

Preparation Time: 5 minutes

Cooking Time: 25 minutes

Servings: 4

Nutrition: Calories: 295 Fat: 8g Carbs: 56g Protein: 6g

Ingredients:

- 1 cup barley
- 1 cup wheat berries
- 2 cups unsweetened almond milk
- 2 cups water
- ½ cup blueberries
- ½ cup pomegranate seeds
- ½ cup hazelnuts, toasted and chopped
- ¼ cup honey

Directions:

- ❖ Take a medium saucepan and place it over medium-high heat. Place barley, almond milk, wheat berries, water and bring to a boil. Reduce the heat to low and simmer for 25 minutes.
- ❖ Divide amongst serving bowls and top each serving with 2 tablespoons blueberries, 2 tablespoons pomegranate seeds, 2 tablespoons hazelnuts, 1 tablespoon honey. Serve and enjoy!

DASH DIET RICE, GRAIN & PASTA RECIPES

21) Anchovies Bucatini

Preparation Time: 15 minutes

Cooking Time: 20 minutes

Servings: 4

Nutrition: Calories: 207.4 Carbs: 31g Protein: 5.1g Fat: 7g

Ingredients:

- 1 tbsp capers, rinsed
- 1 tsp coarsely chopped fresh oregano
- 1 tsp finely chopped garlic
- 12-oz bucatini pasta
- 2 cups coarsely chopped canned no-salt-added whole peeled tomatoes with their juice
- 3 tbsp extra virgin olive oil, divided
- 4 anchovy fillets, chopped
- 8 black Kalamata olives, pitted and sliced into slivers

Directions:

- ❖ Cook bucatini pasta according to package directions. Drain, keep warm, and set aside. On medium fire, place a large nonstick saucepan and heat 2 tbsp oil.
- ❖ Sauté anchovies until it starts to disintegrate. Add garlic and sauté for 15 seconds. Add tomatoes, sauté for 15 to 20 minutes or until no longer watery.
- ❖ Add oregano, capers, and olives. Add pasta, sautéing until heated through. To serve, drizzle pasta with remaining olive oil and enjoy.

22) Zucchini Hot Pasta

Preparation Time: 30 minutes

Cooking Time:

Servings: 4

Nutrition: Carbs: 36g Protein: 9.8g Fats: 5.9g Calories: 234

Ingredients:

- Pasta: 1 ½ cup (after cooking)
- Olive oil: 2 tbsp
- Garlic: 2 cloves minced
- Chickpeas: 1 cup can
- Red onion: 1 small diced
- Bell pepper: 1 cup diced
- Zucchini: 1 cup diced
- Tomatoes: 1 cup diced
- Chili powder: 1 tsp
- Cumin: 1 tsp
- Black pepper: ½ tsp
- Green onions: 2 tbsp chopped

Directions:

- ❖ Cooking Time: pasta as per packet instructions
- ❖ Take a large saucepan and add olive oil and heat on medium flame
- ❖ Include onion and garlic to the pan and Cooking Time: for a minute
- ❖ Now add bell pepper, zucchini, tomatoes, chickpeas, cumin, pepper, and chili powder and stir
- ❖ Cooking Time: for 10 minutes
- ❖ Stir the spoon and add cooked pasta
- ❖ Then cover and Cooking Time: for 5 minutes on low flame and remove from heat
- ❖ Sprinkle green onion on top and serve

23) Arugula Linguine

Preparation Time: 15 minutes

Cooking Time: 20 minutes

Servings: 4

Nutrition: Calories: 274.7 Carbs: 30.9g Protein: 14.6g Fat: 10.3g

Ingredients:

- ¼ cup grated low-fat Parmesan cheese
- ½ cup loosely packed fresh basil leaves, torn
- 12 oz whole wheat linguine
- 2 cups loosely packed baby arugula
- 2 green onions, green parts only, sliced thinly
- 2 tbsp balsamic vinegar
- 2 tbsp extra virgin olive oil
- 3 large vine-ripened tomatoes
- 3 oz low-fat Brie cheese, cubed, rind removed and discarded
- 3 tbsp toasted pine nuts

Directions:

- ❖ Toss together vinegar, oil, onions, Parmesan, basil, arugula, Brie and tomatoes in a large bowl and set aside. Cook linguine following package instructions.
- ❖ Reserve 1 cup of pasta cooking water after linguine is cooked. Drain and discard the rest of the pasta. Do not run under cold water, instead immediately add into bowl of salad.
- ❖ Let it stand for a minute without mixing. Add ¼ cup of reserved pasta water into bowl to make a creamy sauce. Add more pasta water if desired. Toss to mix well. Serve and enjoy.

24) Asian Style Pasta

Preparation Time: 30 minutes

Cooking Time:

Servings: 4

Nutrition: Carbs: 29.5g Protein: 5.4g Fats: 8.05g Calories: 205

Ingredients:

- Pasta: 2 cups (after cooking
- Olive oil: 2 tbsp
- Garlic: 2 cloves minced
- Red onion: 1 small diced
- Bell pepper: 1 cup diced
- Cabbage: 1 cup diced
- Carrot: 1 cup diced
- Soy sauce: 1 tbsp
- Hot sauce: 1 tbsp
- Black pepper: ½ tsp
- Green onions: 2 tbsp

Directions:

- ❖ Cooking Time: pasta as per packet instructions
- ❖ Take a large saucepan and add olive oil and heat on medium flame
- ❖ Include onion and garlic to the pan and Cooking Time: for a minute
- ❖ Now add bell pepper, cabbage, carrot, soy sauce, hot sauce, and pepper and stir for 5 minutes
- ❖ Then add pasta and mix well
- ❖ Then cover and Cooking Time: for 2 minutes on low flame and remove from heat
- ❖ Sprinkle green onion on top and serve

25) Mexican Style Pasta

Preparation Time: 30 minutes

Cooking Time:

Servings: 4

Nutrition: Carbs: 47.5g Protein: 14.8g Fats: 12.4g Calories: 304

Ingredients:

- Pasta: 2 cups (after cooking
- Olive oil: 2 tbsp
- Jalapeño: 1 diced
- Green chili: 2 finely diced
- Garlic: 2 cloves minced
- Red onion: 1 small diced
- Dried oregano: 2 tbsp
- For the gravy:
- Vegetable oil 2 tsp
- Chickpeas: 1 cup rinsed and drained
- Onions: 2 thinly sliced
- Plain flour 1 tbsp
- Water: 250 ml
- Boiled water: 600 ml
- Vegan gravy granules: 2 tbsp

Directions:

- ❖ Cooking Time: pasta as per packet instructions
- ❖ Take a large saucepan and add olive oil and heat on medium flame
- ❖ Include onion and garlic to the pan and Cooking Time: for a minute
- ❖ Add pasta, chili, and jalapeño mix well
- ❖ For the gravy, take a pan and heat oil
- ❖ Add in onions and stir then add water
- ❖ Allow the water to evaporate so that onion caramelized
- ❖ Add in flour and Cooking Time: for a minute and then add gravy granules and boiled water
- ❖ Cooking Time: till the gravy becomes thick and then add chickpeas and simmer for 5 minutes
- ❖ Spread pasta on the serving tray and serve with the chickpeas gravy on top
- ❖ Sprinkle dried oregano from top

26) Shrimp Pasta

Preparation Time: 15 minutes

Cooking Time: 10 minutes

Servings: 4

Nutrition: Calories: 324.9 Carbs: 12g Protein: 43.8g Fat: 11.3g

Ingredients:

- ¼ tsp pepper
- 1 lb. raw shelled shrimp
- 1 lemon, cut into wedges
- 1 tbsp butter
- 1 tbsp olive oil
- 2 5-oz cans chopped clams, drained (reserve 2 tbsp clam juice)
- 2 tbsp dry white wine
- 4 cloves garlic, minced
- 4 cups zucchini, spiraled (use a veggie spiralizer)
- 4 tbsp Parmesan Cheese
- fresh parsley, chopped to garnish

Directions:

- ❖ Ready the zucchini and spiralize with a veggie spiralizer. Arrange 1 cup of zucchini noodle per bowl. Total of 4 bowls.
- ❖ On medium fire, place a large nonstick saucepan and heat oil and butter. For a minute, sauté garlic. Add shrimp and cook for 3 minutes until opaque or cooked.
- ❖ Add white wine, reserved clam juice and clams. Bring to a simmer and continue simmering for 2 minutes or until half of liquid has evaporated. Stir constantly.
- ❖ Season with pepper. Remove from fire and evenly distribute seafood sauce to 4 bowls. Top with a tablespoonful of Parmesan cheese per bowl, serve and enjoy.

27) Chili Macaronis

Preparation Time: 30 minutes

Cooking Time:

Servings: 2

Nutrition: Carbs: 52g Protein: 26.9g Fats: 17.4g Calories: 312

Ingredients:

- Macaronis: 1 cup (after cooking
- Chickpeas: 1 cup rinsed and drained
- Cherry tomatoes: 1 cup diced
- Onions: 1 chopped
- Garlic: 2 cloves
- Vinegar: 3 tbsp
- Olive oil: 2 tbsp
- Tabasco: 4-5 dashes
- Pepper: as per your taste
- Spring onion greens: 3 tbsp chopped

Directions:

- ❖ Take a pan and heat oil
- ❖ Add onion and sauté for 5 minutes
- ❖ Add tomatoes and whole garlic cloves and sauté for 5 minutes and stir
- ❖ Add in vinegar, Tabasco, and a lot pepper
- ❖ Cooking Time: macaroni as per packet instructions and add chickpeas near the end and stir
- ❖ Drain the pasta but keep 2 tablespoons of water and add to tomatoes
- ❖ Add the tomato mixture to the blender and blend
- ❖ Add pasta to the serving tray and mix in tomato sauce
- ❖ Top with spring onion

28) Sea Festival Couscous

Preparation Time: 15 minutes

Cooking Time: 10 minutes

Servings: 4

Nutrition: Calories: 117 Carbs: 11.7g Protein: 11.5g Fat: 3.1g

Ingredients:

- ½ cup whole wheat couscous
- 4 oz small shrimp, peeled and deveined
- 4 oz bay scallops, tough muscle removed
- ¼ cup vegetable broth
- 1 cup freshly diced tomatoes and juice
- Pinch of crumbled saffron threads
- ¼ tsp freshly ground pepper
- ½ tsp fennel seed
- ½ tsp dried thyme
- 1 clove garlic, minced
- 1 medium onion, chopped
- 2 tsp extra virgin olive oil

Directions:

- ❖ Put on medium fire a large saucepan and add oil. Stir in the onion and sauté for three minutes before adding: saffron, pepper, fennel seed, thyme, and garlic.
- ❖ Continue to sauté for another minute. Then add the broth and tomatoes and let boil. Once boiling, reduce the fire, cover and continue to cook for another 2 minutes.
- ❖ Add the scallops and increase fire to medium and stir occasionally and cook for two minutes. Add the shrimp and wait for two minutes more before adding the couscous.
- ❖ Then remove from fire, cover and set aside for five minutes before carefully mixing.

29) Wave of Shrimp and Quinoa

Preparation Time: 15 minutes

Cooking Time: 25 minutes

Servings: 7

Nutrition: Calories: 324.4 Protein: 22g Carbs: 33g Fat: 11.6g

Ingredients:

- 1 lb. large shrimp, peeled, deveined and thawed
- 1 tsp seafood seasoning
- 1 cup frozen green peas
- 1 red bell pepper, cored, seeded & membrane removed, sliced into ½" strips
- ½ cup sliced sun-dried tomatoes, packed in olive oil
- ½ tsp black pepper
- ½ tsp Spanish paprika
- ½ tsp saffron threads (optional turmeric)
- 1 bay leaf
- ¼ tsp crushed red pepper flakes
- 3 cups chicken broth, fat free, low sodium
- 1 ½ cups dry quinoa, rinse well
- 1 tbsp olive oil
- 2 cloves garlic, minced
- 1 yellow onion, diced

Directions:

- ❖ Season shrimps with seafood seasoning. Toss to mix well and refrigerate until ready to use. Prepare and wash quinoa. Set aside.
- ❖ On medium low fire, place a large nonstick skillet and heat oil. Add onions and for 5 minutes sauté until soft and tender.
- ❖ Add paprika, saffron (or turmeric), bay leaves, red pepper flakes, chicken broth and quinoa. Season with pepper. Cover skillet and bring to a boil.
- ❖ Once boiling, lower fire to a simmer and cook until all liquid is absorbed, around ten minutes. Add shrimp, peas and sun-dried tomatoes.
- ❖ For 5 minutes, cover and cook. Once done, turn off fire and for ten minutes allow paella to set while still covered. To serve, remove bay leaf and enjoy with a squeeze of lemon if desired.

30) Cucumber Noodles

Preparation Time: 15minutes

Cooking Time:

Servings: 2

Nutrition: Carbs: 46.8g Protein: 13g Fats: 17.3g Calories: 408

Ingredients:

- Wholewheat noodles: 275g pack
- Sugar snap peas: a handful halved
- Toasted sesame seeds: 1 tbsp
- Cucumber: ½ peeled seeded and chopped
- Sesame oil: 1 tsp
- Red pepper: ½ sliced
- Roughly chopped coriander: a small bunch
- For the Dressing:
- Soy sauce: 2 tsp
- Vinegar: 2 tbsp
- Ginger: 3cm piece grated
- Garlic: 1/2 clove crushed
- Peanut butter: 1 tbsp smooth
- Chili oil: 1 tbsp

Directions:

- ❖ Cooking Time: noodles as per packet instructions
- ❖ Take a bowl and add cooked noodles and pour some sesame oil
- ❖ Add red pepper, cucumber and sugar snaps and mix well
- ❖ Mix all dressing ingredients well, ladle over the noodles
- ❖ Sprinkle some sesame seeds and coriander

31) Spinach and Shrimp Pasta

Preparation Time: 15 minutes

Cooking Time: 0 minutes

Servings: 4

Nutrition: Calories: 151 Carbs: 18.9g Protein: 4.3g Fat: 7.4g

Ingredients:

- 2 cups baby spinach
- 2 tbsp fresh lemon juice
- 2 tbsp extra virgin olive oil
- 3 tbsp drained capers
- ¼ cup chopped fresh basil
- 1 lb. peeled and deveined large shrimp
- 8 oz uncooked spaghetti
- 3 quarts water

Directions:

- ❖ In a pot, bring to boil 3 quarts water. Add the pasta and allow to boil for another eight mins before adding the shrimp and boiling for another three mins or until pasta is cooked.
- ❖ Drain the pasta and transfer to a bowl. Add lemon juice, olive oil, capers and basil while mixing well. To serve, place baby spinach on plate around ½ cup and topped with ½ cup of pasta

32) Tomato Shower Pasta

Preparation Time: 30 minutes

Cooking Time:

Servings: 2

Nutrition: Carbs: 63.8 g Protein: 11.8 g Fats: 8.9 g Calories: 378

Ingredients:

- All-purpose flour: 4 tbsp
- Whole wheat pasta: 1 ¼ cup
- Garlic: 8 large cloves
- Grape tomatoes: 3 cups half
- Shallots: 2 medium diced
- Olive oil
- Black pepper: as per your taste
- Unsweetened plain almond milk: 2 ½ cup

Directions:

- ❖ Preheat the oven to 204C
- ❖ Add half tomatoes to the baking sheet lined with parchment paper
- ❖ Brush with olive oil and bake for 20 minutes
- ❖ Cooking Time: pasta as per packet instructions
- ❖ Prepare sauce side by side, take a pan and add 1 tablespoon of olive oil
- ❖ Add shallot and garlic and stir
- ❖ Sprinkle pepper and mix and Cooking Time: for 4 minutes till it softens
- ❖ Add in flour and mix and add almond milk and again add a pinch of pepper
- ❖ Cooking Time: until thicken and add in garlic
- ❖ Blend the sauce to make it creamier and back to the pan to heat up
- ❖ Now add pasta and top with tomatoes and mix
- ❖ Serve immediately when hot

33) Cheese Festival Spaghetti

Preparation Time: 15 minutes

Cooking Time: 10 minutes

Servings: 6

Nutrition: Calories: 264 Fat: 16.8g Protein: 8.6g Carbs: 22.8g

Ingredients:

- 1 pound (454 g) cooked whole-wheat spaghetti
- 2 tablespoons extra-virgin olive oil
- 4 cloves garlic, minced
- ¾ cup walnuts, toasted and finely chopped
- 2 tablespoons ricotta cheese
- ¼ cup flat-leaf parsley, chopped
- ½ cup grated Parmesan cheese
- Freshly ground pepper, to taste

Directions:

- ❖ Reserve a cup of spaghetti water while cooking the spaghetti. Heat the olive oil in a nonstick skillet over medium-low heat or until shimmering.
- ❖ Add the garlic and sauté for a minute or until fragrant. Pour the spaghetti water into the skillet and cook for 8 more minutes. Turn off the heat and mix in the walnuts and ricotta cheese.
- ❖ Put the cooked spaghetti on a large serving plate, then pour the walnut sauce over. Spread with parsley and Parmesan, then sprinkle with ground pepper. Toss to serve.

34) Brocoli Pasta

Preparation Time: 30 minute

Cooking Time:

Servings: 2

Nutrition: Carbs: 42.5g Protein:13.4g Fats: 10.5g Calories:227.2

Ingredients:

- Pasta: 1 cup cooked
- Long-stemmed broccoli: 1 cup
- Kale: 1 cup
- Olive oil: 1 tbsp
- Peas: 1 cup
- Smoked paprika: ½ tsp

Directions:

- ❖ Cooking Time: pasta as per packet instructions
- ❖ Take a pan and heat olive oil
- ❖ Take a bowl and add broccoli, peas, paprika and mix well and add to the pan
- ❖ Fry on low heat for 20 minutes and turn in between
- ❖ Add kale at the last minutes
- ❖ Mix pasta and season

35) Cauliflower Fettuccine

Preparation Time: 35 minutes

Cooking Time: 30 minutes

Servings: 4

Nutrition: Calories: 288 Fat: 15.9g Protein: 10.1g Carbs: 32.5g

Ingredients:

- Cauliflower Alfredo Sauce:
- 1 tablespoon avocado oil
- ½ yellow onion, diced
- 2 cups cauliflower florets
- 2 garlic cloves, minced
- 1½ teaspoons miso
- 1 teaspoon Dijon mustard
- Pinch of ground nutmeg
- ½ cup unsweetened almond milk
- 1½ tablespoons fresh lemon juice
- 2 tablespoons nutritional yeast
- Ground black pepper, to taste
- Fettuccine:
- 1 tablespoon avocado oil
- ½ yellow onion, diced
- 1 cup broccoli florets
- 1 zucchini, halved lengthwise and cut into ¼-inch-thick half-moons
- Sea salt and ground black pepper, to taste
- ½ cup sun-dried tomatoes, drained if packed in oil
- 8 ounces (227 g) cooked whole-wheat fettuccine
- ½ cup fresh basil, cut into ribbons

Directions:

- ❖ Heat the avocado oil in a nonstick skillet over medium-high heat until shimmering. Add half of the onion to the skillet and sauté for 5 minutes or until translucent.
- ❖ Add the cauliflower and garlic to the skillet. Reduce the heat to low and cook for 8 minutes or until the cauliflower is tender.
- ❖ Pour them in a food processor, add the remaining ingredients for the sauce and pulse to combine well. Set aside.
- ❖ Heat the avocado oil in a nonstick skillet over medium-high heat. Add the remaining half of onion and sauté for 5 minutes or until translucent.
- ❖ Add the broccoli and zucchini. Sprinkle with ground black pepper, then sauté for 5 minutes or until tender.
- ❖ Add the sun-dried tomatoes, reserved sauce, and fettuccine. Sauté for 3 minutes or until well-coated and heated through.
- ❖ Serve the fettuccine on a large plate and spread with basil before serving.

36) Rice Orange

Preparation Time: 15 minutes

Cooking Time: 15 minutes

Servings: 6

Nutrition: Calories: 264 Fat: 7.1g Protein: 5.2g Carbs: 48.9g

Ingredients:

- 1 tablespoon extra-virgin olive oil
- 1 cup chopped onion
- ½ cup shredded carrot
- ½ teaspoon ground cinnamon
- 1 teaspoon ground cumin
- 2 cups brown rice
- 1¾ cups pure orange juice
- ¼ cup water
- ½ cup shelled pistachios
- 1 cup golden raisins
- ½ cup chopped fresh chives

Directions:

- ❖ Heat the olive oil in a saucepan over medium-high heat until shimmering. Add the onion and sauté for 5 minutes or until translucent.
- ❖ Add the carrots, cinnamon, and cumin, then sauté for 1 minutes or until aromatic.
- ❖ Pour int the brown rice, orange juice, and water. Bring to a boil. Reduce the heat to medium-low and simmer for 7 minutes or until the liquid is almost absorbed.
- ❖ Transfer the rice mixture in a large serving bowl, then spread with pistachios, raisins, and chives. Serve immediately.

37) Curry Pecans

Preparation Time: 15 minutes

Cooking Time: 8 minutes

Servings: 4

Nutrition: Calories: 254 Fat: 11.9g Protein: 5.4g Carbs: 34.3g

Ingredients:

- 2 teaspoons extra-virgin olive oil
- 2 leeks, white parts only, sliced
- 1 apple, diced
- 2 cups cooked couscous
- 2 tablespoons curry powder
- ½ cup chopped pecans

Directions:

- ❖ Heat the olive oil in a skillet over medium heat until shimmering. Add the leeks and sauté for 5 minutes or until soft.
- ❖ Add the diced apple and cook for 3 more minutes until tender. Add the couscous and curry powder. Stir to combine. Transfer them in a large serving bowl, then mix in the pecans and serve.

38) *Lemony Farro and Avocado Bowl*

Preparation Time: 15 minutes

Cooking Time: 25 minutes

Servings: 4

Nutrition: Calories: 210 Fat: 11.1g Protein: 4.2g Carbs: 27.9g

Ingredients:

- 1 tablespoon plus 2 teaspoons extra-virgin olive oil, divided
- ½ medium onion, chopped
- 1 carrot, shredded
- 2 garlic cloves, minced
- 1 (6-ounce / 170-g) cup pearled farro
- 2 cups low-sodium vegetable soup
- 2 avocados, peeled, pitted, and sliced
- Zest and juice of 1 small lemon

Directions:

- ❖ Heat 1 tablespoon of olive oil in a saucepan over medium-high heat until shimmering. Add the onion and sauté for 5 minutes or until translucent. Add the carrot and garlic and sauté for 1 minute or until fragrant.
- ❖ Add the farro and pour in the vegetable soup. Bring to a boil over high heat. Reduce the heat to low. Put the lid on and simmer for 20 minutes or until the farro is al dente.
- ❖ Transfer the farro in a large serving bowl, then fold in the avocado slices. Sprinkle with lemon zest, then drizzle with lemon juice and 2 teaspoons of olive oil. Stir to mix well and serve immediately.

39) *Sweet Potatoes Stuffed*

Preparation Time: 15 minutes

Cooking Time: 20 minutes

Servings: 4

Nutrition: Calories: 393 Fat: 7.1g Protein: 10.2g Carbs: 76.9g

Ingredients:

- 2 cups cooked wild rice
- ½ cup dried blueberries
- ½ cup chopped hazelnuts
- ½ cup shredded Swiss chard
- 1 teaspoon chopped fresh thyme
- 1 scallion, white and green parts, peeled and thinly sliced
- Freshly ground black pepper, to taste
- 4 sweet potatoes, baked in the skin until tender

Directions:

- ❖ Preheat the oven to 400°F (205°C). Combine all the ingredients, except for the sweet potatoes, in a large bowl. Stir to mix well.
- ❖ Cut the top third of the sweet potato off length wire, then scoop most of the sweet potato flesh out. Fill the potato with the wild rice mixture, then set the sweet potato on a greased baking sheet.
- ❖ Bake in the preheated oven for 20 minutes or until the sweet potato skin is lightly charred. Serve immediately.

40) *Asparagus and Cherry Tomatoes Blend*

Preparation Time: 15 minutes

Cooking Time: 33 minutes

Servings: 4-6

Nutrition: Calories: 240 Carbs: 26g Fat: 12g Protein: 9g

Ingredients:

- 1 teaspoon Dijon mustard
- 1½ cups whole farro
- 2 ounces feta cheese, crumbled (½ cup)
- 2 tablespoons lemon juice
- 2 tablespoons minced shallot
- 3 tablespoons chopped fresh dill
- 3 tablespoons extra-virgin olive oil
- 6 ounces asparagus, trimmed and cut into 1-inch lengths
- 6 ounces cherry tomatoes, halved
- 6 ounces sugar snap peas, strings removed, cut into 1-inch lengths

Directions:

- ❖ Bring 4 quarts water to boil in a Dutch oven. Put in asparagus, snap peas, and cook until crisp-tender, approximately 3 minutes.
- ❖ Use a slotted spoon to move vegetables to large plate and allow to cool completely, about 15 minutes. Put in farro to water, return to boil, and cook until grains are soft with slight chew, 15 to 30 minutes.
- ❖ Drain farro, spread in rimmed baking sheet, and allow to cool completely, about 15 minutes.
- ❖ Beat oil, lemon juice, shallot, mustard, and ¼ teaspoon pepper together in a big container.
- ❖ Put in vegetables, farro, tomatoes, dill, and ¼ cup feta and toss gently to combine. Sprinkle with pepper to taste. Move to serving platter and drizzle with remaining ¼ cup feta. Serve.

DASH DIET

SIDE & SALAD

RECIPES

41) Avocado Bites

Preparation Time: 25 minutes

Cooking Time:

Servings: 4

Nutrition: Carbs: 5 g Protein: 1 g Fats: 10 g Calories: 110

Ingredients:
- Avocado mashed:1
- Cucumbers:2cut into thick slices
- Lemon: 1 tsp
- Vegan chipotle mayo:2 tbsp
- Spicy roasted chickpeas: ½ pack
- Fresh herbs:3 tbsp

Directions:
- ❖ Add lemon and seasoning to the mashed avocado
- ❖ Place on each cucumber slice and press using chickpeas
- ❖ Top with herbs and mayo and serve

42) Air Fresh Salad with feta

Preparation Time: 15 minutes

Cooking Time: 0 minutes

Servings: 6-8

Nutrition: Calories: 100 Carbs: 5g Fat: 8g Protein: 2g

Ingredients:
- ¼ cup chopped fresh mint
- ¼ cup chopped fresh parsley
- ½ cup pitted kalamata olives, quartered
- ½ red onion, sliced thin
- 1 cup jarred roasted red peppers, rinsed, patted dry, and cut into ½-inch strips
- 1 garlic clove, minced
- 1 teaspoon lemon juice
- 1½ tablespoons red wine vinegar
- 2 cucumbers, peeled, halved along the length, seeded, and sliced thin
- 2 teaspoons minced fresh oregano
- 5 ounces feta cheese, crumbled (1¼ cups)
- 6 large ripe tomatoes, cored, seeded, and cut into ½-inch-thick wedges
- 6 tablespoons extra-virgin olive oil

Directions:
- ❖ Beat oil, vinegar, oregano, lemon juice, garlic together in a big container. Put in cucumbers and onion, toss to coat, and allow to sit for 20 minutes.
- ❖ Put in tomatoes, red peppers, olives, parsley, and mint to a container with cucumber-onion mixture and toss to combine.
- ❖ Move salad to wide, shallow serving bowl or platter and drizzle with feta. Serve instantly.

43) Broccoli Salad with a hot touch

Preparation Time: 45 minutes

Cooking Time:

Servings: 2

Nutrition: Carbs: 10.5 g Protein:2.6g Fats: 7.5g Calories: 133

Ingredients:
- Broccoli: 2 cups cut in big florets
- Hot sauce: 2 tbsp
- Rice vinegar: 1 tbsp
- Pepper: as per your taste
- Sliced red pepper: 1 cup sliced
- Olive oil: 1 tbsp

Directions:
- ❖ Preheat the oven 200C
- ❖ Add broccoli to the baking sheet and sprinkle seasoning and brush with olive oil
- ❖ Roast for 25 minutes till it turns golden and soft
- ❖ Take a small bowl and combine hot sauce, vinegar, and pepper
- ❖ Remove broccoli from oven and brush with this dressing and Cooking Time: in the oven again for 10 minutes
- ❖ Add to the serving bowl and serve with red pepper
- ❖ Serve as the side dish

44) Mushroom Salad

Preparation Time: 15 minutes

Cooking Time: 0 minutes

Servings: 6

Nutrition: Calories: 70 Carbs: 1g Fat: 3g Protein: 1g

Ingredients:
- ¼ cup extra-virgin olive oil
- ½ cup fresh parsley leaves
- 1 shallot, halved and sliced thin
- 1½ tablespoons lemon juice
- 2 ounces Parmesan cheese, shaved
- 2 tablespoons chopped fresh tarragon
- 4 celery ribs, sliced thin, plus ½ cup celery leaves
- 8 ounces cremini mushrooms, trimmed and sliced thin

Directions:
- ❖ Beat oil and lemon juice together in a big container. Put in mushrooms and shallot, toss to coat, and allow to sit for about ten minutes.
- ❖ Put in sliced celery and leaves, Parmesan, parsley, and tarragon to mushroom-shallot mixture and toss to combine. Serve.

45) Green Hummus

Preparation Time: 10 minutes

Cooking Time:

Servings: 4 as a side dish

Nutrition: Carbs: 25.8g Protein: 10.7g Fats: 18.6g Calories: 296

Ingredients:

- Chickpeas: 2 cups tin drained and rinsed
- Baby spinach: 1 cup
- Tahini: 3 tbsp
- Garlic: 1 clove
- Lemon: 2 tbsp
- Extra-virgin olive oil: 3 tbsp, plus extra to serve

Directions:

- ❖ Blend baby spinach, chickpeas, tahini, olive oil, and garlic together in a blender
- ❖ Add in lemon juice and mix
- ❖ Add to the serving bowl and top with extra olive oil

46) Special Cucumber Salad

Preparation Time: 1-3 hours & 15 minutes

Cooking Time: 0 minutes

Servings: 4

Nutrition: Calories: 187 Carbs: 29g Fat: 7g Protein: 6g

Ingredients:

- 1/8 teaspoon red pepper flakes, plus extra for seasoning
- ¼ cup rice vinegar
- 1 tablespoon lemon juice
- 1 tablespoon sesame seeds, toasted
- 2 tablespoons toasted sesame oil
- 2 teaspoons sugar
- 3 cucumbers, peeled, halved along the length, seeded, and sliced ¼ inch thick

Directions:

- ❖ Toss cucumbers with 1 tablespoon salt using a colander set over big container. Weight cucumbers with 1 gallon-size zipper-lock bag filled with water; drain for 1 to three hours. Wash and pat dry.
- ❖ Beat vinegar, oil, lemon juice, sesame seeds, sugar, and pepper flakes together in a big container. Put in cucumbers and toss to coat. Serve at room temperature or chilled.

47) Red and Yellow Salad

Preparation Time: 25 minute

Cooking Time:

Servings: 4

Nutrition: Carbs: 29.9g Protein: 5.9g Fats: 10g Calories: 227

Ingredients:

- Red bell Pepper: 1
- Yellow bell pepper: 1
- Smoked Paprika: ½ tsp
- Potatoes: 3 medium
- Mushrooms: 8 oz
- Yellow Onion: 1
- Zucchini: 1
- Cumin Powder: ½ tsp
- Garlic Powder: ½ tsp
- Cooking oil: 2 tbsp (optional)

Directions:

- ❖ Heat a large pan on medium flame, add oil and put the sliced potatoes
- ❖ Cooking Time: the potatoes till they change color
- ❖ Cut the rest of the vegetables and add all the spices
- ❖ Cooked till veggies are soften

48) Romantic Green Salad

Preparation Time: 15 minutes

Cooking Time: 0 minutes

Servings: 4

Nutrition: Calories: 170 Carbs: 0g Fat: 8g Protein: 22g

Ingredients:

- ½ cup chopped fresh parsley
- ½ cup pitted kalamata olives, chopped
- ½ small red onion, chopped fine
- 1 (15-ounce) can chickpeas, rinsed
- 1 cucumber, peeled, halved along the length, seeded, and cut into ½-inch pieces
- 1 garlic clove, minced
- 1 romaine lettuce heart (6 ounces), cut into ½-inch pieces
- 10 ounces grape tomatoes, quartered
- 3 tablespoons extra-virgin olive oil
- 3 tablespoons red wine vinegar
- 4 ounces feta cheese, crumbled (1 cup)

Directions:

- ❖ Toss cucumber and tomatoes and allow to drain using a colander for about fifteen minutes.
- ❖ Beat vinegar and garlic together in a big container. Whisking continuously, slowly drizzle in oil.
- ❖ Put in cucumber-tomato mixture, chickpeas, olives, onion, and parsley and toss to coat. Allow to sit for minimum 5 minutes or maximum 20 minutes.
- ❖ Put in lettuce and feta and gently toss to combine. Serve.

49) Red Hummus

Preparation Time: 10 minutes

Cooking Time:

Servings: 4 as a side dish

Nutrition: Carbs: 27.1g Protein: 9.8g Fats: 18.7g Calories: 302

Ingredients:
- Chickpeas: 2 cups can rinsed and drained
- Red bell pepper: 1 cup diced
- Tahini: 3 tbsp
- Garlic: 1 clove
- Lemon: 2 tbsp
- Extra-virgin olive oil: 3 tbsp, plus extra to serve
- Cayenne pepper: 1 tsp

Directions:
- ❖ Blend all ingredient together in a blender except lemon juice.
- ❖ Add in lemon juice and mix
- ❖ Serve!

50) Herbed Cream Cheese Toast

Preparation Time: 10 minutes

Cooking Time: 5 minutes

Servings: 2

Nutrition: Calories: 194 Fat: 8g Carbs: 2g Protein: 12g

Ingredients:
For the herbed cream cheese:
- ¼ cup cream cheese, at room temperature
- 2 tablespoons chopped fresh flat-leaf parsley
- 2 tablespoons chopped fresh chives or sliced scallion
- ½ teaspoon garlic powder

For the toast:
- 2 slices bread
- 4 ounces smoked salmon
- Small handful microgreens or sprouts
- 1 tablespoon capers, drained and rinsed
- ¼ small red onion, very thinly sliced

Directions:
- ❖ In a medium bowl, combine the cream cheese, parsley, chivesb and garlic powder. Using a fork, mix until combined. Chill until ready to use.
- ❖ Toast the bread until golden. Spread the herbed cream cheese over each piece of toast, then top with the smoked salmon. Garnish with the microgreens, capers, and red onion.

51) Peas Salad

Preparation Time: 5minutes

Cooking Time:

Servings: 2

Nutrition: Carbs: 10g Protein: 5g Fats: 6.5g Calories: 133

Ingredients:
- Frozen peas: 1 cup can washed and drained
- Pepper: as per your taste
- Cashew cream: ½ cup

Directions:
- ❖ Combine all the ingredients
- ❖ Serve as the side dish

52) Extravagant mix Broccoli Salad

Preparation Time: 25 minutes

Cooking Time: 0 minutes

Servings: 6

Nutrition: Calories 90 Fat 9 g Carbs 4 g Protein 2 g

Ingredients:
- 3 cups broccoli, chopped
- 1 tbsp apple cider vinegar
- ½ cup Greek yogurt
- 2 tbsp sunflower seeds
- 3 bacon slices, cooked and chopped
- 1/3 cup onion, sliced
- ¼ tsp stevia

Directions:
- ❖ In a mixing bowl, mix together broccoli, onion, and bacon. In a small bowl, mix together yogurt, vinegar, and stevia and pour over broccoli mixture. Stir to combine.
- ❖ Sprinkle sunflower seeds on top of the salad. Store salad in the refrigerator for 30 minutes. Serve and enjoy.

53) Veggie Bite

Preparation Time: 30 minutes

Cooking Time:

Servings: 2

Nutrition: Carbs: 21.5g Protein:9.4g Fats: 9.55g Calories: 127.2

Ingredients:
- Long-stemmed broccoli: 1 cup
- Kale: 1 cup
- Olive oil: 1 tbsp
- Peas: 1 cup
- Smoked paprika: ½ tsp

Directions:
- ❖ Take a pan and heat olive oil
- ❖ Take a bowl and add broccoli, peas, paprika and mix well and add to the pan
- ❖ Fry on low heat for 20 minutes and turn in between
- ❖ Add kale at the last minutes
- ❖ Serve as a salad with the main dish

54) Shrimp Salad

Preparation Time: 15 minutes

Cooking Time: 0 minutes

Servings: 2

Nutrition: Calories: 314 Protein,: 26g Carbs: 15g Fats: 9g

Ingredients:

- 14 ounces of jumbo cooked shrimp, peeled and deveined; chopped
- 4 ½ ounces of avocado, diced
- 1 ½ cup of tomato, diced
- ¼ cup of chopped green onion
- ¼ cup of jalapeno with the seeds removed, diced fine
- 1 teaspoon of olive oil
- 2 tablespoons of lime juice
- 1 tablespoon of chopped cilantro

Directions:

- ❖ Get a small bowl and combine green onion, olive oil, lime juice, pepper, a pinch of salt. Wait for about 5 minutes for all of them to marinate and mellow the flavor of the onion.
- ❖ Get a large bowl and combined chopped shrimp, tomato, avocado, jalapeno. Combine all of the ingredients, add cilantro, and gently toss.

55) Pure Remember Canada

Preparation Time: 20 minutes

Cooking Time:

Servings: 2

Nutrition: Carbs: 7.5g Protein: 0.4g Fats: 0.1g Calories: 33

Ingredients:

- Rice: 250g
- Maple syrup: 2 tsp
- Water: 500 ml

Directions:

- ❖ Toast rice in the pan lightly and soak overnight in 250ml water
- ❖ Add maple syrup, rice, and 250ml water to the blender and blend till smoothen
- ❖ Strain and discard the puree
- ❖ Shake before serving

56) Mahi-Mahi Jicama

Preparation Time: 20 minutes

Cooking Time: 10 minutes

Servings: 4

Nutrition: Calories: 320 Protein: 44g Carbs: 10g Fat: 11 g

Ingredients:

- 1 teaspoon each for pepper and salt, divided
- 1 tablespoon of lime juice, divided
- 2 tablespoon + 2 teaspoons of extra virgin olive oil
- 4 raw mahi-mahi fillets, which should be about 8 oz. each
- ½ cucumber which should be thinly cut into long strips (it should yield about 1 cup)
- 1 jicama, which should be thinly cut into long strips (it should yield about 3 cups)
- 1 cup of alfalfa sprouts
- 2 cups of coarsely chopped watercress

Directions:

- ❖ Combine ½ teaspoon of both pepper and salt, 1 teaspoon of lime juice, and 2 teaspoons of oil in a small bowl. Then brush the mahi-mahi fillets all through with the olive oil mixture.
- ❖ Grill the mahi-mahi on medium-high heat until it becomes done in about 5 minutes, turn it to the other side, and let it be done for about 5 minutes.
- ❖ For the slaw, combine the watercress, cucumber, jicama, and alfalfa sprouts in a bowl. Now combine ½ teaspoon of both pepper and salt, 2 teaspoons of lime juice, and 2 tablespoons of extra virgin oil in a small bowl. Drizzle it over slaw and toss together to combine.

57) Chili Potatoes

Preparation Time: 35 minutes

Cooking Time:

Servings: 2

Nutrition: Carbs: 26 g Protein: 3g Fats: 7.2g Calories: 178

Ingredients:

- Olive oil: 1 tbsp
- Potatoes: 2 cups cut like fries
- Pepper: as per your taste
- Red chili flakes: 1 tsp

Directions:

- ❖ Preheat the oven 200C
- ❖ Add potatoes to the baking sheet and sprinkle seasoning and brush with olive oil
- ❖ Roast for 25 minutes till it turns golden and soft
- ❖ Remove from the oven and sprinkle red chili flakes
- ❖ Serve as the side dish

58) Boneless Salad

Preparation Time: 5 minutes

Cooking Time: 25 minutes

Servings: 4

Nutrition: Calories: 340 Protein: 45g Carbs: 9g Fat: 4 g

Ingredients:

For Chicken:

- 1 ¾ lb. boneless, skinless chicken breast
- 1 ½ tablespoon of butter, melted
- For Mediterranean salad:
- 1 cup of sliced cucumber
- 6 cups of romaine lettuce, that is torn or roughly chopped
- 10 pitted Kalamata olives
- 1 pint of cherry tomatoes
- 1/3 cup of reduced-fat feta cheese
- ¼ teaspoon each of pepper and salt (or lesser)
- 1 small lemon juice (it should be about 2 tablespoons)

Directions:

❖ Preheat your oven or grill to about 350F. Season the chicken with butter. Roast or grill chicken until it reaches an internal temperature of 1650F in about 25 minutes.

❖ Once your chicken breasts are cooked, remove and keep aside to rest for about 5 minutes before you slice it.

❖ Combine all the salad ingredients you have and toss everything together very well. Serve the chicken with Mediterranean salad.

59) The Secret of Parsnip

Preparation Time: 35 minutes

Cooking Time:

Servings: 4

Nutrition: Carbs: 24g Protein: 1.6g Fats: 3.9g Calories: 141

Ingredients:

- Parsnips: 4 thickly sliced
- Olive oil: 1 tbsp
- For the Zhoug:
- Flat-leaf parsley: ½ cup chopped
- Coriander: ½ cup chopped
- Vinegar: 1 tbsp
- Green chili: 1 chopped
- Garlic: ½ clove chopped
- Ground cumin: ½ tsp

Directions:

❖ Preheat the oven to 200C
❖ Take a baking sheet and place parsnips
❖ Brush oil
❖ Bake for 25-30 minutes till they tender
❖ In the meanwhile, add all the zhoug ingredients to the food processor and blend
❖ Add 3-4 tablespoons of water if needed
❖ Serve roasted parsnips with zhoug

60) Awesome Shrimp Cocktail

Preparation Time: 35 minutes

Cooking Time: 35 minutes

Servings: 8

Nutrition: Calories: 580 Carbs: 16 g Fat: 46 g Protein: 24 g

Ingredients:

- 2 cups mayonnaise
- 6 plum tomatoes, seeded and finely chopped
- 1/4 cup ketchup
- 1/4 cup lemon juice
- 2 cups seedless red and green grapes, halved
- 1 tablespoon. Worcestershire sauce
- 2 lbs. peeled and deveined cooked large shrimp
- 2 celery ribs, finely chopped
- 3 tablespoons. minced fresh tarragon or 3 teaspoon dried tarragon
- shredded 2 of cups romaine
- papaya or 1/2 cup peeled chopped mango
- parsley or minced chives

Directions:

❖ Combine Worcestershire sauce, lemon juice, ketchup and mayonnaise together in a small bowl. Combine tarragon, celery and shrimp together in a large bowl.

❖ Put in 1 cup of dressing toss well to coat. Scoop 1 tablespoon. of the dressing into 8 cocktail glasses.

❖ Layer each glass with 1/4 cup of lettuce, followed by 1/2 cup of the shrimp mixture, 1/4 cup of grapes, 1/3 cup of tomatoes and finally 1 tablespoon. of mango.

❖ Spread the remaining dressing over top; sprinkle chives on top. Serve immediately.

DASH DIET

MAIN RECIPES

61) Veggie Meatballs

Preparation Time: 5 minutes

Cooking Time: 25 minutes

Servings: 4

Nutrition: Calories:506, Fat: 45.6g, Carbs:11g, Protein:19g

Ingredients:

- 3 lb ground tofu
- 1 medium yellow onion, finely chopped
- 2 green bell peppers, deseeded and chopped
- 3 garlic cloves, minced
- 2 tbsp melted butter
- 1 tsp dried parsley
- 2 tbsp hot sauce
- Ground black pepper to taste
- 1 tbsp red curry powder
- 3 tbsp olive oil

Directions:

- ❖ Preheat the oven to 400 F and grease a baking sheet with cooking spray.
- ❖ In a bowl, combine the tofu, onion, bell peppers, garlic, butter, parsley, hot sauce, black pepper, and curry powder. With your hands, form 1-inch tofu ball from the mixture and place on the greased baking sheet.
- ❖ Drizzle the olive oil over the meat and bake in the oven until the tofu ball brown on the outside and Cooking Time: within, 20 to 25 minutes.
- ❖ Remove the dish from the oven and plate the tofu ball.
- ❖ Garnish with some scallions and serve warm on a bed of spinach salad with herbed vegan paneer cheese dressing.

62) Parsley Chicken

Preparation Time: 10 minutes

Cooking Time: 20 minutes

Servings: 8

Nutrition: Calories 292 Fat 13 g Carbs 8.9 g Protein 34.3 g

Ingredients:

- 2 lb. chicken thighs
- 1/2 cup olives
- 28 oz can tomato, diced
- 1 1/2 tsp dried oregano
- 2 tsp dried parsley
- 1/2 tsp ground coriander powder
- 1/4 tsp chili pepper
- 1 tsp onion powder
- 1 tsp paprika
- 2 cups onion, chopped
- 2 tbsp olive oil
- Pepper

Directions:

- ❖ Add oil into the inner pot of instant pot and set the pot on sauté mode. Add chicken and cook until browned. Transfer chicken on a plate. Add onion and sauté for 5 minutes.
- ❖ Add all spices, tomatoes, and cook for 2-3 minutes. Return chicken to the pot and stir everything well. Seal pot with lid and cook on high for 8 minutes.
- ❖ Once done, release pressure using quick release. Remove lid. Add olives and stir well. Serve and enjoy.

63) Zucchini Tofu

Preparation Time: 5minutes

Cooking Time: 12minutes

Servings: 4

Nutrition: Calories:79, Fat:6.2g, Carbs:5g, Protein:2g

Ingredients:

- 2 tbsp olive oil
- 1 medium white onion, chopped
- 1 garlic clove, minced
- 2 (14 ozblocks firm tofu, pressed and cubed
- 1 medium red bell pepper, deseeded and sliced
- 6 medium zucchinis, spiralized
- Black pepper to taste
- ¼ cup basil pesto, olive oil based
- 2/3 cup grated parmesan cheese
- ½ cup shredded mozzarella cheese
- Toasted pine nuts to garnish

Directions:

- ❖ Heat the olive oil in a medium pot over medium heat; sauté the onion and garlic until softened and fragrant, 3 minutes.
- ❖ Add the tofu and Cooking Time: until golden on all sides then pour in the bell pepper and Cooking Time: until softened, 4 minutes.
- ❖ Mix in the zucchinis, pour the pesto on top, and season with black pepper. Cooking Time: for 3 to 4 minutes or until the zucchinis soften a little bit. Turn the heat off and carefully stir in the parmesan cheese.
- ❖ Dish into four plates, share the mozzarella cheese on top, garnish with the pine nuts, and serve warm.

64) Greek Chicken

Preparation Time: 10 minutes

Cooking Time: 8 minutes

Servings: 6

Nutrition: Calories 472 Fat 15.5 g Carbs 22.7 g Protein 57.6 g

Ingredients:

- 2 1/2 lb. chicken breasts, skinless and boneless
- 14 oz can artichokes
- 1/2 cup olives, pitted
- 3/4 cup prunes
- 1 tbsp capers
- 1 1/2 tbsp garlic, chopped
- 3 tbsp red wine vinegar
- 2 tsp dried oregano
- 1/3 cup wine
- Pepper

Directions:

- ❖ Add all ingredients except chicken into the instant pot and stir well. Add chicken and mix well. Seal pot with lid and cook on high for 8 minutes.
- ❖ Once done, allow to release pressure naturally for 10 minutes then release remaining using quick release. Remove lid. Serve and enjoy.

65) Countryside Pie

Preparation Time: 12minutes

Cooking Time: 43minutes

Servings: 4

Nutrition: Calories:120, Fat: 9.2g, Carbs:7g, Protein:5g

Ingredients:

- For the piecrust:
- ¼ cup almond flour + extra for dusting
- 3 tbsp coconut flour
- ¼ cup butter, cold and crumbled
- 3 tbsp erythritol
- 1 ½ tsp vanilla extract
- 4 whole eggs
- For the filling:
- 2 tbsp butter
- 1 medium yellow onion
- 2 garlic cloves, minced
- 2 cups mixed mushrooms, chopped
- 1 green bell pepper, deseeded and diced
- 1 cup green beans, cut into 3 pieces each
- Salt and black pepper to taste
- ¼ cup coconut creaminutes
- 1/3 cup vegan sour creaminutes
- ½ cup almond milk
- 2 eggs, lightly beaten
- ¼ tsp nutmeg powder
- 1 tbsp chopped parsley
- 1 cup grated parmesan cheese

Directions:

- ❖ For the pastry crust:
- ❖ Preheat the oven to 350 F and grease a pie pan with cooking spray
- ❖ In a large bowl, mix the almond flour and coconut flour.
- ❖ Add the butter and mix with an electric hand mixer until crumbly. Add the erythritol and vanilla extract until mixed in. Then, pour in the eggs one after another while mixing until formed into a ball.
- ❖ Flatten the dough a clean flat surface, cover in plastic wrap, and refrigerate for 1 hour.
- ❖ After, lightly dust a clean flat surface with almond flour, unwrap the dough, and roll out the dough into a large rectangle, ½ - inch thickness and fit into a pie pan.
- ❖ Pour some baking beans onto the pastry and bake in the oven until golden. Remove after, pour the beans, and allow cooling.
- ❖ For the filling:
- ❖ Meanwhile, melt the butter in a skillet and sauté the onion and garlic until softened and fragrant, 3 minutes. Add the mushrooms, bell pepper, green beans and black pepper; Cooking Time: for 5 minutes.
- ❖ In a medium bowl, beat the coconut cream, vegan sour cream, milk, and eggs. Season with black pepper and nutmeg. Stir in the parsley and cheese.
- ❖ Spread the mushroom mixture in the baked pastry and spread the cheese filling on top. Place the pie in the oven and bake for 30 to 35 minutes or until a toothpick inserted into the pie comes out clean and golden on top.
- ❖ Remove, let cool for 10 minutes, slice, and serve with roasted tomato salad.

66) Piccata Style Chicken

Preparation Time: 10 minutes

Cooking Time: 41 minutes

Servings: 6

Nutrition: Calories 406 Fat 17 g Carbs 1.2 g Protein 57 g

Ingredients:

- 8 chicken thighs, bone-in, and skin-on
- 2 tbsp fresh parsley, chopped
- 1 tbsp olive oil
- 3 tbsp capers
- 2 tbsp fresh lemon juice
- 1/2 cup chicken broth
- 1/4 cup dry white wine
- 1 tbsp garlic, minced

Directions:

- ❖ Add oil into the inner pot of instant pot and set the pot on sauté mode. Add garlic and sauté for 1 minute. Add wine and cook for 5 minutes or until wine reduced by half.
- ❖ Add lemon juice and broth and stir well. Add chicken and seal pot with the lid and select manual and set a timer for 30 minutes.
- ❖ Once done, release pressure using quick release. Remove lid. Remove chicken from pot and place on a baking tray. Broil chicken for 5 minutes. Add capers and stir well. Garnish with parsley and serve.

67) Salmon & Pesto

Preparation Time: 5 minutes

Cooking Time: 10 minutes

Servings: 2

Nutrition: Calories 316, 20g fat, 29g protein

Ingredients:

- 10 ounces (283 g) salmon fillet
- 2 tablespoons prepared pesto sauce
- 1 large fresh lemon, sliced
- Cooking spray

Directions:

- ❖ Preheat the grill to medium-high heat. Spray the grill grates with cooking spray.
- ❖ Season the salmon well. Spread the pesto sauce on top.
- ❖ Make a bed of fresh lemon slices about the same size as the salmon fillet on the hot grill, and place the salmon on top of the lemon slices. Put any additional lemon slices on top of the salmon.
- ❖ Grill the salmon for 10 minutes.
- ❖ Serve hot.

68) Tofu of Green Beans and Avocado

Preparation Time: 10minutes

Cooking Time: 22 minutes

Servings: 4

Nutrition: Calories:503, Fat: 19.9g, Carbs:18g, Protein:19g

Ingredients:

- For the tofu chops:
- 2 tbsp avocado oil
- 4 slices firm tofu
- Salt and ground black pepper to taste
- For the green beans and avocado sauté:
- 2 tbsp avocado oil
- 1 ½ cups green beans
- 2 large avocados, halved, pitted, and chopped
- Ground black pepper to taste
- 6 green onions, chopped
- 1 tbsp freshly chopped parsley

Directions:

- ❖ For the tofu chops:
- ❖ Heat the avocado oil in a medium skillet, season the tofu with salt and black pepper, and fry in the oil on both sides until brown, and cooked through, 12 to 15 minutes. Transfer to a plate and set aside in a warmer for serving.
- ❖ For the green beans and avocado sauté:
- ❖ Heat the avocado oil in a medium skillet, add and sauté the green beans until sweating and slightly softened, 10 minutes. Mix in the avocados (don't worry if they mash up a bit), season with black pepper, and the half of the green onions. Warm the avocados for 2 minutes. Turn the heat off.
- ❖ Dish the sauté into serving plates, garnish with the remaining green onions and parsley, and serve with the tofu chops.

69) Amazing Lemon Chicken

Preparation Time: 10 minutes

Cooking Time: 18 minutes

Servings: 4

Nutrition: Calories 220 Fat 8.9 g Carbs 7.8 g Protein 26.4 g

Ingredients:

- 8 chicken drumsticks, skin-on
- 2 tbsp balsamic vinegar
- 2/3 cup can tomato, diced
- 6 garlic cloves
- 1 tsp lemon zest, grated
- 1 tsp dried thyme
- 1/4 tsp red pepper flakes
- 1 1/2 onions, cut into wedges
- 1 tbsp olive oil
- Pepper

Directions:

- ❖ Add oil into the inner pot of instant pot and set the pot on sauté mode. Add onion and 1/2 tsp salt and sauté for 2-3 minutes.
- ❖ Add chicken, garlic, lemon zest, red pepper flakes, and thyme and mix well. Add vinegar and tomatoes and stir well.
- ❖ Seal pot with lid and cook on high for 15 minutes. Once done, release pressure using quick release. Remove lid. Stir well and serve.

70) Cauli Quinoa with chili

Preparation Time: 30 minutes

Cooking Time:

Servings: 4

Nutrition: Calories 414 Fats 20g Carbs 45.9g Protein 20.8g

Ingredients:

- 1 tbsp olive oil
- 1 lb extra firm tofu, pressed and cut into 1-inch cubes
- Black pepper to taste
- 1 medium yellow onion, finely diced
- ½ cup cauliflower florets
- 1 jalapeño pepper, minced
- 2 garlic cloves, minced
- 1 tbsp red chili powder
- 1 tsp cumin powder
- 1 (8 ozcan sweet corn kernels, drained
- 1 (8 ozcan lima beans, rinsed and drained
- 1 cup quick-cooking quinoa
- 1 (14 ozcan diced tomatoes
- 2 ½ cups vegetable broth
- 1 cup grated homemade plant-based cheddar cheese
- 2 tbsp chopped fresh cilantro
- 2 limes, cut into wedges for garnishing
- 1 medium avocado, pitted, sliced and peeled

Directions:

- ❖ Heat olive oil in a pot and Cooking Time: the tofu until golden brown, 5 minutes. Season with pepper, and mix in onion, cauliflower, and jalapeño pepper. Cooking Time: until the vegetables soften, 3 minutes. Stir in garlic, chili powder, and cumin powder; Cooking Time: for 1 minute.
- ❖ Mix in sweet corn kernels, lima beans, quinoa, tomatoes, and vegetable broth. Simmer until the quinoa absorbs all the liquid, 10 minutes. Fluff quinoa. Top with the plant-based cheddar cheese, cilantro, lime wedges, and avocado. Serve warm.

71) Chicken & Mushrooms Italian Blend

Preparation Time: 10 minutes

Cooking Time: 21 minutes

Servings: 6

Nutrition: Calories 244 Fat 13.5 g Carbs 4.1 g Protein 26 g

Ingredients:

- 1 lb. chicken breasts, skinless, boneless, & cut into 1-inch pieces
- 1/4 cup olives, sliced
- 2 oz feta cheese, crumbled
- 1/4 cup sherry
- 1 cup chicken broth
- 1 tsp Italian seasoning
- 12 oz mushrooms, sliced
- 2 celery stalks, diced
- 1 tsp garlic, minced
- 1/2 cup onion, chopped
- 2 tbsp olive oil
- Pepper

Directions:

- ❖ Add oil into the inner pot of instant pot and set the pot on sauté mode. Add mushrooms, celery, garlic, and onion and sauté for 5-7 minutes.
- ❖ Add chicken, Italian seasoning, pepper, and stir well and cook for 4 minutes. Add sherry and broth and stir well. Seal pot with lid and cook on high for 10 minutes.
- ❖ Once done, allow to release pressure naturally for 10 minutes then release remaining using quick release. Remove lid. Add olives and feta cheese and stir well. Serve and enjoy.

72) Crumbled Tempeh Rice

Preparation Time: 50 minutes

Cooking Time:

Servings: 4

Nutrition: Calories 216 Fats 13.9g Carbs 13.8g Protein 12.7g

Ingredients:

- 2 tbsp olive oil
- 1 ½ cups crumbled tempeh
- 1 tsp Creole seasoning
- 2 red bell peppers, deseeded and sliced
- 1 cup brown rice
- 2 cups vegetable broth
- 1 lemon, zested and juiced
- 1 (8 oz can black beans, drained and rinsed
- 2 chives, chopped
- 2 tbsp freshly chopped parsley

Directions:

- ❖ Heat the olive oil in a medium pot and Cooking Time: in the tempeh until golden brown, 5 minutes.
- ❖ Season with the Creole seasoning and stir in the bell peppers. Cooking Time: until the peppers slightly soften, 3 minutes.
- ❖ Stir in the brown rice, vegetable broth, and lemon zest.
- ❖ Cover and Cooking Time: until the rice is tender and all the liquid is absorbed, 15 to 25 minutes.
- ❖ Mix in the lemon juice, beans, and chives. Allow warming for 3 to 5 minutes and dish the food.
- ❖ Garnish with the parsley and serve warm.

73) Oats Burgers

Preparation Time: 20 minutes

Cooking Time:

Servings: 4

Nutrition: Calories 589

Fats 17.7g Carbs 80.9g Protein 27.9g

Ingredients:

- 3 (15 oz cans black beans, drained and rinsed
- 2 tbsp whole-wheat flour
- 2 tbsp quick-cooking oats
- ¼ cup chopped fresh basil
- 2 tbsp pure barbecue sauce
- 1 garlic clove, minced
- Black pepper to taste
- 4 whole-grain hamburger buns, split
- For topping:
- Red onion slices
- Tomato slices
- Fresh basil leaves
- Additional barbecue sauce

Directions:

- ❖ In a medium bowl, mash the black beans and mix in the flour, oats, basil, barbecue sauce, garlic, and black pepper until well combined. Mold 4 patties out of the mixture and set aside.
- ❖ Heat a grill pan to medium heat and lightly grease with cooking spray.
- ❖ Cooking Time: the bean patties on both sides until light brown and cooked through, 10 minutes.
- ❖ Place the patties between the burger buns and top with the onions, tomatoes, basil, and some barbecue sauce.
- ❖ Serve warm.

74) Trout with Shiitake Mushrooms

Preparation Time: 10 minutes

Cooking Time: 25 minutes

Servings: 2

Nutrition: Calories 453, 20g fat, 49g protein

Ingredients:

- 2 (8-ounce) whole trout fillets
- 1 tablespoon extra-virgin olive oil
- 1/8 teaspoon black pepper
- 1 small onion, thinly sliced
- ½ red bell pepper
- 1 poblano pepper
- 2 or 3 shiitake mushrooms, sliced
- 1 lemon, sliced

Directions:

- ❖ Set oven to 425°F (220°C). Coat baking sheet with nonstick cooking spray.
- ❖ Rub both trout fillets, inside and out, with the olive oil. Season with pepper.
- ❖ Mix together the onion, bell pepper, poblano pepper, and mushrooms in a large bowl. Stuff half of this mix into the cavity of each fillet. Top the mixture with 2 or 3 lemon slices inside each fillet.
- ❖ Place the fish on the prepared baking sheet side by side. Roast in the preheated oven for 25 minutes
- ❖ Pullout from the oven and serve on a plate.

75) Rice with soy chorizo

Preparation Time: 50 minutes

Cooking Time:

Servings: 4

Nutrition: Calories 253 Fats 8.4g Carbs 32.7g Protein 15.5g

Ingredients:

- 2 tbsp olive oil
- 2 cups chopped soy chorizo
- 1 tsp taco seasoning
- 2 green bell peppers, deseeded and sliced
- 1 cup brown rice
- 2 cups vegetable broth
- ¼ cup salsa
- 1 lemon, zested and juiced
- 1 (8 ozcan pinto beans, drained and rinsed
- 1 (7 ozcan sweet corn kernels, drained
- 2 green onions, chopped
- 2 tbsp freshly chopped parsley

Directions:

- ❖ Heat the olive oil in a medium pot and Cooking Time: the soy chorizo until golden brown, 5 minutes.
- ❖ Season with the taco seasoning and stir in the bell peppers; Cooking Time: until the peppers slightly soften, 3 minutes.
- ❖ Stir in the brown rice, vegetable broth, salt, salsa, and lemon zest.
- ❖ Close the lid and Cooking Time: the food until the rice is tender and all the liquid is absorbed, 15 to 25 minutes.
- ❖ Mix in the lemon juice, pinto beans, corn kernels, and green onions. Allow warming for 3 to 5 minutes and dish the food.
- ❖ Garnish with the parsley and serve warm.

76) Trout & Shallots

Preparation Time: 10 minutes

Cooking Time: 20 minutes

Servings: 2

Nutrition: Calories 344, 18g fat, 21g protein

Ingredients:

- Shallots:
- 1 teaspoon almond butter
- 2 shallots, thinly sliced
- Trout:
- 1 tablespoon almond butter
- 2 (4-ounce / 113-g) trout fillets
- 3 tablespoons capers
- ¼ cup freshly squeezed lemon juice
- ¼ teaspoon salt
- Dash freshly ground black pepper
- 1 lemon, thinly sliced

Directions:

- ❖ Situate skillet over medium heat, cook the butter, shallots, and salt for 20 minutes, stirring every 5 minutes.
- ❖ For Trout
- ❖ Meanwhile, in another large skillet over medium heat, heat 1 teaspoon of almond butter.
- ❖ Add the trout fillets and cook each side for 3 minutes, or until flaky. Transfer to a plate and set aside.
- ❖ In the skillet used for the trout, stir in the capers, lemon juice, and pepper, then bring to a simmer. Whisk in the remaining 1 tablespoon of almond butter. Spoon the sauce over the fish.
- ❖ Garnish the fish with the lemon slices and caramelized shallots before serving.

77) Light Melts

Preparation Time: 5 minutes

Cooking Time: 4 minutes

Servings: 2

Nutrition: Calories 244, 10g fat, 30g protein

Ingredients:

- 1 (5-oz) can chunk light tuna packed in water
- 2 tablespoons plain Greek yogurt
- 2 tablespoons finely chopped celery
- 1 tablespoon finely chopped red onion
- 2 teaspoons freshly squeezed lemon juice
- 1 large tomato, cut into ¾-inch-thick rounds
- ½ cup shredded Cheddar cheese

Directions:

- ❖ Preheat the broiler to High.
- ❖ Stir together the tuna, yogurt, celery, red onion, lemon juice, and cayenne pepper in a medium bowl.
- ❖ Place the tomato rounds on a baking sheet. Top each with some tuna salad and Cheddar cheese.
- ❖ Broil for 3 to 4 minutes until the cheese is melted and bubbly. Cool for 5 minutes before serving.

78) Quinoa Burger with a Sweet Touch

Preparation Time: 35 minutes

Cooking Time:

Servings: 4

Nutrition: Calories 290 Fats 6.2g Carbs 50.2g Protein 12g

Ingredients:

- 1 cup quick-cooking quinoa
- 1 tbsp olive oil
- 1 shallot, chopped
- 2 tbsp chopped fresh celery
- 1 garlic clove, minced
- 1 (15 ozcan pinto beans, drained and rinsed
- 2 tbsp whole-wheat flour
- ¼ cup chopped fresh basil
- 2 tbsp pure maple syrup
- Black pepper to taste
- 4 whole-grain hamburger buns, split
- 4 small lettuce leaves for topping
- ½ cup tofu mayonnaise for topping

Directions:

- ❖ Cooking Time: the quinoa with 2 cups of water in a medium pot until liquid absorbs, 10 to 15 minutes.
- ❖ Meanwhile, heat the olive oil in a medium skillet over medium heat and sauté the shallot, celery, and garlic until softened and fragrant, 3 minutes.
- ❖ Transfer the quinoa and shallot mixture to a medium bowl and add the pinto beans, flour, basil, maple syrup, and black pepper. Mash and mold 4 patties out of the mixture and set aside.
- ❖ Heat a grill pan to medium heat and lightly grease with cooking spray. Cooking Time: the patties on both sides until light brown, compacted, and cooked through, 10 minutes. Place the patties between the burger buns and top with the lettuce and tofu mayonnaise. Serve warm.

79) Masala Mushroom Biryani

Preparation Time: 50 minutes

Cooking Time: 4

Servings:

Nutrition: Calories 255

Fats 16.8g| Carbs 25.6g Protein 5.8g

Ingredients:

- 1 cup brown rice
- 2 cups water
- 3 tbsp plant butter
- 3 medium white onions, chopped
- 6 garlic cloves, minced
- 1 tsp ginger puree
- 1 tbsp turmeric powder + more for
- dusting
- ¼ tsp cinnamon powder
- 2 tsp garam masala
- ½ tsp cardamom powder
- ½ tsp cayenne powder
- ½ tsp cumin powder
- 1 tsp smoked paprika
- 3 large tomatoes, diced
- 2 green chilies, deseeded and minced
- 1 tbsp tomato puree
- 1 cup chopped cremini mushrooms
- 1 cup chopped mustard greens
- 1 cup plant-based yogurt for topping

Directions:

- ❖ Melt the butter in a large pot and sauté the onions until softened, 3 minutes. Mix in the garlic, ginger, turmeric, cardamom powder, garam masala, cardamom powder, cayenne pepper, cumin powder and paprika. Stir-fry while cooking until the fragrant, 1 to 2 minutes.
- ❖ Stir in the tomatoes, green chili, tomato puree, and mushrooms. Once boiling, mix in the rice and cover with water. Cover the pot and Cooking Time: over medium heat until the liquid absorbs and the rice is tender, 15-20 minutes.
- ❖ Open the lid and fluff in the mustard greens and half of the parsley. Dish the food, top with the coconut yogurt, garnish with the remaining parsley, and serve warm.

80) Sweet Salmon

Preparation Time: 5 minutes

Cooking Time: 8 minutes

Servings: 4

Nutrition: Calories: 454 Fat: 17.3g Protein: 65.3g Carbs: 9.7g

Ingredients:

- ½ cup balsamic vinegar
- 1 tablespoon honey
- 4 (8-ounce / 227-g) salmon fillets
- Freshly ground pepper, to taste
- 1 tablespoon olive oil

Directions:

- ❖ Heat a skillet over medium-high heat. Combine the vinegar and honey in a small bowl. Season the salmon fillets with the freshly ground pepper; brush with the honey-balsamic glaze.
- ❖ Add olive oil to the skillet, and sear the salmon fillets, cooking for 3 to 4 minutes on each side until lightly browned and medium rare in the center. Let sit for 5 minutes before serving.

DASH DIET
SOUP RECIPES

81) Mix Veggie Soup

Preparation Time: 50 minutes

Cooking Time:

Servings: 4

Nutrition: Carbs: 45.25 g Protein: 10.4 g Fats: 8.7 g Calories: 264

Ingredients:

- Potatoes: 2 cups peeled and diced
- Black beans can: 2 cups rinsed and drained
- Kale: 1 cup chopped
- Onion: 1 medium finely chopped
- Garlic: 4 cloves minced
- Olive oil: 2 tsp
- Fresh rosemary leaves: 2 tbsp minced
- Vegetable broth: 4 cups
- Ground black pepper: as per your taste

Directions:

- ❖ Take a large saucepan and add oil
- ❖ On a medium heat, add onions and Cooking Time: for 6-8 minutes
- ❖ A dd rosemary and garlic and stir for a minute
- ❖ Add potatoes with pepper and sauté for two minutes
- ❖ Pour vegetable broth and bring to boil
- ❖ Lower the heat and Cooking Time: for 30
- ❖ minutes till potatoes become soft
- ❖ By using the back of spoon mash a few potatoes
- ❖ Add kale and beans to the soup and again Cooking Time: for 5 minutes till they tender
- ❖ Remove the soup from heat and season with salt and pepper

82) Thai Basil-Scented soup

Preparation Time: 15 minutes

Cooking Time: 8 hours

Servings: 12

Nutrition: Calories: 255 Carbs: 1.2g Fats: 17.6g Proteins: 25.2g

Ingredients:

- 1 lemongrass stalk, cut into large chunks
- 5 thick slices of fresh ginger
- 1 whole chicken
- 20 fresh basil leaves
- 1 lime, juiced

Directions:

- ❖ Place the chicken, 10 basil leaves, lemongrass, ginger and water into the slow cooker. Cook for about 8 hours on low and dish out into a bowl. Stir in fresh lime juice and basil leaves to serve.

83) Veggie Curry Soup

Preparation Time: 35 minutes

Cooking Time:

Servings: 3

Nutrition: Carbs: 44.5g Protein: 21.7g Fats: 19,8g Calories: 312.66

Ingredients:

- Black beans: 1 cup can
- Cashew nuts: ½ cup
- Spinach: 2 cups chopped
- Onion: 1 medium
- Freshly grated ginger: 2 tbsp
- Curry powder: 1 tbsp mild
- Vegetable broth: 2 cups
- Olive oil: 2 tbsp
- Lemon juice: as per your taste
- Garlic: 3 cloves
- Fresh coriander: 2 tbsp

Directions:

- ❖ Take a large pan and add olive oil
- ❖ Add onion and garlic and fry for a minute and add curry powder and ginger
- ❖ Continue frying for 5 minutes to make onion soft
- ❖ Add spinach and vegetable broth and Cooking Time: on a medium flame for 10 minutes
- ❖ Now blend with the hand blender
- ❖ Add sliced cashews and black beans
- ❖ Add water if needed and simmer for 5 minutes
- ❖ Serve with lemon juice and fresh coriander on top

84) Special Chicken Soup

Preparation Time: 15 minutes

Cooking Time: 6 hours & 15 minutes

Servings: 6

Nutrition: Calories: 261 Carbs: 2g Fats: 20g Proteins: 14.1g

Ingredients:

- 2 pounds chicken breast, skinless
- 1/3cup onion
- 1 tablespoon olive oil
- 14 ounces chicken bone broth
- ½ cup olive oil
- 4 cups chicken stock
- ¼ cup lemon juice
- 5 ounces baby kale leaves

Directions:

- ❖ Season chicken with black pepper. Heat olive oil over medium heat in a large skillet and add seasoned chicken.
- ❖ Reduce the temperature and cook for about 15 minutes. Shred the chicken and place it in the crock pot. Process the chicken broth and onions in a blender and blend until smooth.
- ❖ Pour into crock pot and stir in the remaining ingredients. Cook on low for about 6 hours, stirring once while cooking.

85) Vegetable Party Soup

Preparation Time: 45 minutes

Cooking Time:

Servings: 4

Nutrition: Carbs: 43.5g Protein: 7.72g Fats: 8.6g Calories: 248.5 Kcal

Ingredients:

- Potatoes: 3 cups chopped
- Black beans: 1 cup can rinsed and drained
- Celery: 4 stalks sliced
- Fresh rosemary: 3 sprigs
- Carrots: 4 large sliced
- Vegetable oil: 2 tbsp
- Garlic: 2 cloves minced
- Shallots: 2 small diced
- Vegetable broth: 4 cups
- Broccoli: 1 cup florets
- Kale: 1 cup chopped
- Black pepper: as per your need

Directions:

- ❖ Take a large pot and add oil to it
- ❖ On the medium flame, add shallots, garlic, celery and onion
- ❖ Add pepper to them and stir for 5 minutes till they turn brown
- ❖ Now add potatoes and broccoli and again season with pepper and sauté for two minutes
- ❖ Pour vegetable broth and add rosemary and bring the mixture to boil
- ❖ Lower the heat now and let it Cooking Time: for 20 minutes till potatoes soften
- ❖ Include kale and black beans; stir, cover, and Cooking Time: for 5 minutes
- ❖ Adjust the overall seasoning and add pepper if needed

86) Special Mushrooms Soup

Preparation Time: 15 minutes

Cooking Time: 1 hour & 30 minutes

Servings: 6

Nutrition: Calories: 250 Carbs: 6.4g Fats: 8.9g Proteins: 35.1g

Ingredients:

- 5 chicken thighs
- 12 cups water
- 1 tablespoon adobo seasoning
- 4 celery ribs
- 1 yellow onion
- 1½ teaspoons whole black peppercorns
- 6 sprigs fresh parsley
- 2 teaspoons coarse sea salt
- 2 carrots
- 6 mushrooms, sliced
- 2 garlic cloves
- 1 bay leaf
- 3 sprigs fresh thyme

Directions:

- ❖ Put water, chicken thighs, carrots, celery ribs, onion, garlic cloves and herbs in a large pot. Bring to a boil and reduce the heat to low.
- ❖ Cover the pot and simmer for about 30 minutes. Dish out the chicken and shred it, removing the bones. Put the bones back into the pot and simmer for about 20 minutes.
- ❖ Strain the broth, discarding the chunks and put the liquid back into the pot. Bring it to a boil and simmer for about 30 minutes.
- ❖ Put the mushrooms in the broth and simmer for about 10 minutes. Dish out to serve hot.

87) Homemade Soup

Preparation Time: 40 minutes

Cooking Time:

Servings: 2

Nutrition: Carbs: 24.35g Protein: 4.7g Fats: 7.95g Calories: 167.5Kcal

Ingredients:

- Corns: 2 cups can
- Broccoli: 1 cup
- Potato: 1 cup
- Spinach: 3 cups
- Garlic: 4 cloves
- Ginger root: 1 tbsp grated
- Spring onion: 4
- Turmeric: 1 tsp
- Lemon juice: 2 tbsp
- Coriander: ¼ cup chopped
- Ground coriander: 1 tsp
- Ground cumin: 1 tsp
- Pepper: as per your taste
- Olive oil: 2 tbsp
- Vegetable broth: 4 cups

Directions:

- ❖ In a large saucepan and heat olive oil
- ❖ Crush garlic and chop white part of the green onion and sauté for a minute
- ❖ Add coriander, cumin, ginger and turmeric and fry for a minute
- ❖ Peel and dice potatoes, wash spinach, and separate broccoli florets and add to the pan
- ❖ Sauté them for 5 minutes and add vegetable broth
- ❖ Boil, and heat on low flame for 20 minutes
- ❖ Blend the soup well and season with pepper
- ❖ Top with corns, lemon juice, and coriander leaves

88) Celery Soup with Chicken

Preparation Time: 15 minutes

Cooking Time: 0 minutes

Servings: 10

Nutrition: Calories: 215 Carbs: 7.1g Fats: 8.5g Proteins: 26.4g

Ingredients:

- 1½ tablespoons curry powder
- 3 cups celery root, diced
- 2 tablespoons Swerve
- 10 cups chicken broth
- 5 cups chicken, chopped and cooked
- ¼ cup apple cider
- ½ cup sour cream
- ¼ cup fresh parsley, chopped
- 2 tablespoons butter
- Black pepper, to taste

Directions:

- ❖ Combine the broth, butter, chicken, curry powder, celery root and apple cider in a large soup pot. Bring to a boil and simmer for about 30 minutes.
- ❖ Stir in Swerve, sour cream, fresh parsley and black pepper. Dish out and serve hot.

89) Soup Italian Taste

Preparation Time: 40 minutes

Cooking Time:

Servings: 2

Nutrition: Carbs: 30.8g Protein: 12.7g Fats: 15.2g Calories: 323.2

Ingredients:

- Brown lentils: 1 cup
- Crushed tomatoes: 2 cups
- Onion: 1 diced
- Ginger: 1 tbsp paste
- Garlic: 1 tbsp paste
- Vegetable oil: 2 tbsp
- Water: 4 cups
- Italian herb seasoning: 1 tbsp
- Pepper: as per your taste

Directions:

- ❖ Take a large saucepan and add oil on a medium flame
- ❖ Add onion and ginger and garlic paste and sauté for 3-4 minutes
- ❖ Pour water and bring to boil
- ❖ Add lentils and bring to boil
- ❖ Lower the heat to medium and Cooking Time: for 20 minutes with partial cover
- ❖ Now add crushed tomatoes to the lentils along with herb seasoning and pepper
- ❖ Cooking Time: on low flame for 15 minutes
- ❖ Add the mixture to the high speed blender to make puree
- ❖ Add pepper to augment taste

90) Cream Chese ann Chicken Soup

Preparation Time: 15 minutes

Cooking Time: 0 minutes

Servings: 4

Nutrition: Calories: 444 Carbs: 4g Fats: 34g Proteins: 28g

Ingredients:

- 2 tablespoons parsley
- 2 celery stalks, chopped
- 6 tablespoons butter
- 1 cup heavy whipping cream
- 4 cups chicken, cooked and shredded
- 4 tablespoons ranch dressing
- ¼ cup yellow onions, chopped
- 8 oz cream cheese
- 8 cups chicken broth
- 7 hearty bacon slices, crumbled

Directions:

- ❖ Heat butter in a pan and add chicken. Cook for about 5 minutes and add 1½ cups water. Cover and cook for about 10 minutes.
- ❖ Put the chicken and rest of the ingredients into the saucepan except parsley and cook for about 10 minutes. Top with parsley and serve hot.

91) Unforgettable Tomatoes Soup

Preparation Time: 30 minutes

Cooking Time:

Servings: 2

Nutrition: Carbs: 40g Protein: 13.87g Fats: 18.05g Calories: 385.7

Ingredients:

- Cannellini beans: 1 cup can
- Tomatoes: 1 cup chunks
- Tomatoes: 1 cup can
- Tomato paste: 2 tbsp
- Oregano: 2 tbsp dried
- Onion: 1 (finely chopped)
- Garlic: 3 cloves (crushed
- Fresh basil: 1 small bunch
- Vegetable broth: 4 cups
- Pepper: as per your taste
- Olive oil: 2 tbsp

Directions:

- ❖ Take a large saucepan, heat olive oil in it
- ❖ Add onion and garlic in it
- ❖ Include tomato chunks, can chopped tomatoes, and tomato paste and combine them all together
- ❖ Now add vegetable broth, oregano and fresh basil
- ❖ Bring the mixture to boil and then lower the heat to medium and Cooking Time: for 15 minutes
- ❖ Use the hand blender to blend the soup content and season with pepper
- ❖ Rinse, dry, and roast the cannellini beans
- ❖ Add these beans on top of the soup and serve hot

92) Chicken Soup with a Rosemary Touch

Preparation Time: 15 minutes

Cooking Time: 0 minutes

Servings: 6

Nutrition: Calories: 357 Carbs: 3.3g Fats: 7g Proteins: 66.2g

Ingredients:

- 3 pounds chicken
- 4 quarts water
- 4 stalks celery
- 1/3 large red onion
- 1 large carrot
- 3 garlic cloves
- 2 thyme sprigs
- 2 rosemary sprigs
- Black pepper, to taste

Directions:

- ❖ Put water and chicken in the stock pot on medium high heat. Bring to a boil and allow it to simmer for about 10 minutes.
- ❖ Add onion, garlic, celery and pepper and simmer on medium low heat for 30 minutes. Add thyme and carrots and simmer on low for another 30 minutes.
- ❖ Dish out the chicken and shred the pieces, removing the bones. Return the chicken pieces to the pot and add rosemary sprigs. Simmer for about 20 minutes at low heat and dish out to serve.

93) Chickpeas Soup

Preparation Time: 25 minutes

Cooking Time:

Servings: 2

Nutrition: Carbs: 24.03g Protein: 12.16g Fats: 19,86g Calories: 309

Ingredients:

- Chickpeas: 1 cup can
- Cashew nuts: ½ cup
- Spinach: 2 cups chopped
- Onion: 1 medium
- Freshly grated ginger: 2 tbsp
- Curry powder: 1 tbsp mild
- Vegetable broth: 2 cups
- Olive oil: 2 tbsp
- Lemon juice: as per your taste
- Garlic: 3 cloves
- Fresh coriander: 2 tbsp

Directions:

- ❖ Take a large pan and add olive oil
- ❖ Add onion and garlic and fry for a minute and add curry powder and ginger
- ❖ Continue frying for 5 minutes to make onion soft
- ❖ Add spinach and vegetable broth and Cooking Time: on a medium flame for 10 minutes
- ❖ Now blend with the hand blender and add sliced cashews and chickpeas
- ❖ Add water if needed and simmer for 5 minutes
- ❖ Serve with lemon juice and fresh coriander on top

94) Chicken Noodle

Preparation Time: 15 minutes

Cooking Time: 0 minutes

Servings: 6

Nutrition: Calories: 226 Carbs: 3.5g Fats: 8.9g Proteins: 31.8g

Ingredients:

- 1 onion, minced
- 1 rib celery, sliced
- 3 cups chicken, shredded
- 3 eggs, lightly beaten
- 1 green onion, for garnish
- 2 tablespoons coconut oil
- 1 carrot, peeled and thinly sliced
- 2 teaspoons dried thyme
- 2½ quarts homemade bone broth
- ¼ cup fresh parsley, minced
- Black pepper, to taste

Directions:

- ❖ Heat coconut oil over medium-high heat in a large pot and add onions, carrots, and celery. Cook for about 4 minutes and stir in the bone broth, thyme and chicken.
- ❖ Simmer for about 15 minutes and stir in parsley. Pour beaten eggs into the soup in a slow steady stream.
- ❖ Remove soup from heat and let it stand for about 2 minutes. Season with black pepper and dish out to serve.

95) Corn Soup

Preparation Time: 45 minutes

Cooking Time:

Servings: 4

Nutrition: Carbs: 12.9 g Protein: 5.6 g Fats: 8.5 g Calories: 162 Kcal

Ingredients:

- Corn on the cob: 2
- Dried ancho chili: 1
- Onion: 1 finely chopped
- Vegetable stock: 1 liter
- Celery: 2 sticks finely chopped
- Ground cumin: 2 tsp
- Roasted red peppers: 4 chopped
- Garlic: 3 cloves finely chopped
- Sweet smoked paprika: 2 tsp
- Limes: 2 - 1 juice and other wedged to serve
- Vegetable oil: 2 tbsp
- Coriander: a small bunch chopped

Directions:

- ❖ Take a bowl and add ancho chili and pour boiling water from the top
- ❖ Leave the mixture for 10 minutes and then remove stem and seed
- ❖ Take a pan and heat oil in it and add celery and onion and Cooking Time: for 10 minutes
- ❖ Add all the spices and Cooking Time: for a minute
- ❖ Include now ancho chili, vegetable stock, and pepper and Cooking Time: for 15 minutes
- ❖ Season with salt and blend the mixture
- ❖ In the meanwhile, on a light heat Cooking Time: corns in the pan lightly brushed with pepper, and oil
- ❖ Cooking Time: the cobs for 10 minutes and then remove from heat
- ❖ Use a sharp knife to remove corns and add to the soup Sprinkle coriander on top and serve with lime juice

96) Mushrooms Cabbage Soup

Preparation Time: 15 minutes

Cooking Time: 26 minutes

Servings: 8

Nutrition: Calories: 184 Carbs: 4.2g Fats: 13.1g Proteins: 12.6g

Ingredients:

- 2 celery stalks
- 2 garlic cloves, minced
- 4 oz. butter
- 6 oz. mushrooms, sliced
- 2 tablespoons onions, dried and minced
- 8 cups chicken broth
- 1 medium carrot
- 2 cups green cabbage, sliced into strips
- 2 teaspoons dried parsley
- ¼ teaspoon black pepper
- 1½ rotisserie chickens, shredded

Directions:

- ❖ Melt butter in a large pot and add celery, mushrooms, onions and garlic into the pot. Cook for about 4 minutes and add broth, parsley, carrot and black pepper.
- ❖ Simmer for about 10 minutes and add cooked chicken and cabbage. Simmer for an additional 12 minutes until the cabbage is tender. Dish out and serve hot.

97) Potatoes and Carrot Special Soup

Preparation Time: 45 minutes

Cooking Time:

Servings: 2

Nutrition: Carbs: 38.32g Protein: 10.89g Fats: 18.83g Calories: 346

Ingredients:

- Chickpeas: 1 cup can
- Almonds: ½ cup
- Potatoes: 1 cup
- Carrots: 1 cup
- Parsnips: 1 cup
- Onion: 1 large
- Curry powder: 1 tbsp mild
- Tomato paste: 1 tbsp
- Garlic: 3 cloves crushed
- Grated ginger: 2 tbsp
- Turmeric: 1 tsp
- Ground coriander: 1 tsp
- Ground cumin: 1 tsp
- Vegetable broth: 3 cups
- Lemon juice: 2 tbsp
- Fresh coriander: 3 tbsp
- Olive oil: 2 tbsp
- Pepper: as per your taste

Directions:

- ❖ In a large saucepan, add olive oil and heat on medium flame
- ❖ Add the chopped onion, garlic, grated ginger, ground cumin, ground coriander, curry powder, turmeric, and tomato paste
- ❖ Sauté for a minute or two
- ❖ Peel the veggies and dice them and add to the pan and stir for 5 minutes
- ❖ Now add vegetable broth and bring the mixture to boil and cover and heat for 20 minutes
- ❖ With the hand blender, blend the soup and season with pepper
- ❖ Rinse and drain chickpeas and add to the soup
- ❖ Add fresh coriander, almonds, and lemon juice on top and serve hot

98) Festival Sesame and Mushroom Broth

Preparation Time: 25 minutes

Cooking Time:

Servings: 2

Nutrition: Carbs: 27g Protein: 10.2g Fats: 11.2g Calories:188

Ingredients:

- Chickpeas: 1 cup can rinsed and drained
- Mushrooms: 2 cups
- Spring onions: 6
- Tomato sauce: 2 tbsp
- Garlic: 2 cloves crushed
- Ginger root: 2 tbsp crushed
- Sesame seeds: 4 tbsp
- Sesame oil: 1 tbsp
- Pepper: as per your need
- Tamari: 2 tbsp
- Water: 2 cups

Directions:

- ❖ Chop spring onion and reserve its green part and cut mushrooms in half
- ❖ Take a large saucepan and add sesame oil
- ❖ Add the white part of the spring onion to the pan and sauté for a minute
- ❖ Add tomato paste, ginger and garlic and fry again for a minute
- ❖ Add water and fresh mushrooms and chickpeas
- ❖ Cooking Time: for 10 minutes on medium flame and season with pepper
- ❖ Add sesame seeds and tamari sauce and boil for two minutes
- ❖ Serve hot with spring onion sprinkled on top

99) *Chicken and Spinach Soup*

Preparation Time: 5 minutes

Cooking Time: 35 minutes

Servings: 2

Nutrition: Calories: 185, Carbs: 23.8 g, Protein: 10.1 g, Fat: 5.2 g

Ingredients:

- 1 tablespoon virgin olive oil
- 1 red onion (chopped)
- 1 garlic clove (minced)
- 1 celery stalk (chopped)
- 1 cup spinach (fresh, finely chopped)
- 1 tablespoon lemon juice (fresh squeezed)
- 2x 16-ounce cans white kidney beans (drained, rinsed)
- 2 cups chicken broth (or a 14-ounce can of low-sodium chicken broth)
- ¼ teaspoon thyme (dried)
- ½ teaspoon black pepper
- 1 ½ cups water

Directions:

❖ Place a large saucepan on your stove. Add the virgin olive oil to your pan and turn the heat to medium-high. Add the celery, chopped onions, and minced garlic to the pan and allow them to cook for 5 minutes.

❖ Add the white kidney beans, chicken broth, water, thyme, and black pepper to the saucepan.

❖ Allow the liquid to come to a boil, then reduce heat to medium-low and let the soup simmer for 15 minutes.

❖ Transfer two cups of the bean and vegetables from the saucepan to a bowl. Use a slotted spoon to get as little of the liquid as possible. Set the bowl to the side.

❖ Use an emulsion blender to blend the remaining soup mixture in the saucepan. You want to get a nice smooth consistency.

❖ If you do not have an emulsion blender you can use a regular stand-alone blender. Just work in batches to blend everything. Once everything has been thoroughly blended, return back to your saucepan.

❖ Add the 2 cups of beans and vegetable mixture that you removed earlier back into the soup. Bring the soup back up to a boil, stirring occasionally.

❖ Add in the spinach to the soup; after 2 minutes it should begin to wilt.

❖ Turn the heat all the way off, and then stirs in the lemon juice just before serving.

100) *Cheddar Soup*

Preparation Time: 10 minutes

Cooking Time: 25 minutes

Servings: 2

Nutrition: 95 calories 5.4g protein 6.1g carbs, fat 15,7 g

Ingredients:

- ¼ cup long-grain rice
- 4 cups chicken stock
- ½ cup Cheddar cheese, peas
- ¼ teaspoon ground black pepper
- ½ teaspoon Italian seasonings

Directions:

❖ Heat a saucepan with the stock.

❖ Add all ingredients except Cheddar cheese and bring the soup to boil.

❖ Then add cheese and stir it well.

❖ Cook the soup for 5 minutes over the low heat.

DASH DIET
SNACK RECIPES

101) *Hot Blend Chips*

Preparation Time: 10 minutes

Cooking Time: 14 hours

Servings: 10

Nutrition: Calories: 191 Cal Fat: 12 g Carbs: 16 g Protein: 9 g

Ingredients:
- 2 bunches of curly kale
- 2 cups cashews, soaked, drained
- 1/2 cup chopped red bell pepper
- 1 teaspoon garlic powder
- 2 tablespoons red chili powder
- 1/2 teaspoon smoked paprika
- 1/2 cup nutritional yeast
- 1 teaspoon cayenne
- 3 tablespoons lemon juice
- 3/4 cup water

Directions:
- ❖ Place all the ingredients except for kale in a food processor and pulse for 2 minutes until smooth.
- ❖ Place kale in a large bowl, pour in the blended mixture, mix until coated, and dehydrate for 14 hours at 120 degrees F until crispy.
- ❖ If dehydrator is not available, spread kale between two baking sheets and bake for 90 minutes at 225 degrees F until crispy, flipping halfway.
- ❖ When done, let chips cool for 15 minutes and then serve.

102) *Grains Sweet Bit*

Preparation Time: 10 minutes

Cooking Time: 10 minutes

Servings: 2

Nutrition: Calories: 415, Protein: 13.9g, Carbs: 54.4g, Fat: 16.9g

Ingredients:
- ½ oz. chia seeds
- 1 tbsp. pure maple syrup
- 1 c. coconut milk
- 1 tsp. ground cinnamon
- 3 diced peaches
- 2/3 c. granola

Directions:
- ❖ Find a small bowl and add the chia seeds, maple syrup, and coconut milk.
- ❖ Stir well, then cover and pop into the fridge for at least one hour.
- ❖ Find another bowl, add the peaches and sprinkle with the cinnamon. Pop to one side
- ❖ When it's time to serve, take two glasses, and pour the chia mixture between the two.
- ❖ Sprinkle the granola over the top, keeping a tiny amount to one side to use to decorate later.
- ❖ Top with the peaches and top with the reserved granola and serve.

103) *Chickpeas Hummus*

Preparation Time: 5 minutes

Cooking Time: 0 minute

Servings: 4

Nutrition: Calories: 122.7 Cal Fat: 4.1 g Carbs: 17.8 g Protein: 5.1 g

Ingredients:
- 1/4 cup sun-dried tomatoes, without oil
- 1 ½ cups cooked chickpeas
- 1 teaspoon minced garlic
- 2 tablespoons sesame oil
- 1 tablespoon lemon juice
- 1 tablespoon olive oil
- 1/4 cup of water

Directions:
- ❖ Place all the ingredients in a food processor and process for 2 minutes until smooth.
- ❖ Tip the hummus in a bowl, drizzle with more oil, and then serve straight away.

104) *Special Almond Smoothie*

Preparation Time: 10 minutes

Cooking Time: 1 minutes

Servings: 2

Nutrition: Calories: 230, Carbs: 20 g, Fat: 8.1 g, Protein: 21.6 g

Ingredients:
- 1 c. almond milk
- 1 c. blueberries
- 4 ice cubes
- 1 scoop vanilla protein powder
- 1 tbsp. almond butter
- 1 tbsp. chia seeds

Directions:
- ❖ Use a blender to mix the almond butter, vanilla protein powder, chia seeds, almond milk, ice cubes and blueberries together until the consistency is smooth.

105) Mushrooms Swimming

Preparation Time: 10 minutes

Cooking Time: 7 minutes

Servings: 6

Nutrition: Calories: 103 Fat: 9 g Carbs: 2 g Protein: 1 g

Ingredients:

- 12 ounces small button mushrooms
- 1 teaspoon minced garlic
- 1/4 teaspoon dried thyme
- 1/2 teaspoon dried basil
- 1/2 teaspoon red pepper flakes
- 1/4 teaspoon dried oregano
- 1/2 teaspoon maple syrup
- 1/4 cup apple cider vinegar
- 1/4 cup and 1 teaspoon olive oil
- 2 tablespoons chopped parsley

Directions:

- ❖ Take a skillet pan, place it over medium-high heat, add 1 teaspoon oil and when hot, add mushrooms and Cooking Time: for 5 minutes until golden brown.
- ❖ Meanwhile, prepare the marinade and for this, place remaining ingredients in a bowl and whisk until combined.
- ❖ When mushrooms have cooked, transfer them into the bowl of marinade and toss until well coated.
- ❖ Serve straight away

106) Delicious Salmon Muffins

Preparation Time: 10 minutes

Cooking Time: 15 minutes

Servings: 2

Nutrition: Calories: 93, Fat: 6g, Protein: 8g, Carbs: 1g

Ingredients:

- 4 eggs
- 1/3 c. milk
- Pepper
- 1½ oz. smoked salmon
- 1 tbsp. chopped chives
- Green onions, optional

Directions:

- ❖ Preheat the oven to 356 degrees Fahrenheit and grease 6 muffin tin holes with a small amount of olive oil.
- ❖ Place the eggs, milk, and a pinch of pepper into a small bowl and lightly beat to combine.
- ❖ Divide the egg mixture between the 6 muffin holes, then divide the salmon between the muffins and place into each hole, gently pressing down to submerge in the egg mixture, chopped
- ❖ Sprinkle each muffin with chopped chives and place in the oven for about 8-10 minutes or until just set.
- ❖ Leave to cool for about 5 minutes before turning out and storing in an airtight container in the fridge.

107) Veggie Taco

Preparation Time: 5 minutes

Cooking Time: 15 minutes

Servings: 1

Nutrition: Calories: 187 Cal Fat: 9 g Carbs: 16.3 g Protein: 10.4 g

Ingredients:

- 1 tortilla, whole wheat
- 1/4 cup diced roasted red peppers
- 1 cup baby spinach
- 1/3 teaspoon minced garlic
- ¼ teaspoon ground black pepper
- 1/4 teaspoon olive oil
- 1/4 cup hummus
- Oil as needed

Directions:

- ❖ Place a large pan over medium heat, add oil and when hot, add red peppers and garlic, season with black pepper and Cooking Time: for 3 minutes until sauté.
- ❖ Then stir in spinach, Cooking Time: for 1 minute, remove the pan from heat and
- ❖ transfer the mixture in a bowl.
- ❖ Prepare quesadilla and for this, spread hummus on one-half of the tortilla, then spread spinach mixture on it, cover the filling with the other half of the tortilla and Cooking Time: in a pan for 3 minutes per side until browned.
- ❖ When done, cut the quesadilla into wedges and serve.

108) Nachos Mediterranean Style

Preparation Time: 5 Minutes

Cooking Time: 10 Minutes

Servings: 4

Nutrition: Calories: 140 Carbs: 19g Fat: 7g Protein: 2g

Ingredients:

- 4-ounce restaurant-style corn tortilla chips
- 1 medium green onion, thinly sliced (about 1 tbsp.)
- 1 (4 ounces) package finely crumbled feta cheese
- 1 finely chopped and drained plum tomato
- 2 tbsp Sun-dried tomatoes in oil, finely chopped
- 2 tbsp Kalamata olives

Directions:

- ❖ Mix an onion, plum tomato, oil, sun-dried tomatoes, and olives in a small bowl.
- ❖ Arrange the tortillas chips on a microwavable plate in a single layer topped evenly with cheese—microwave on high for one minute.
- ❖ Rotate the plate half turn and continue microwaving until the cheese is bubbly. Spread the tomato mixture over the chips and cheese and enjoy.

109) Bruschetta Fusion

Preparation Time: 10 minutes

Cooking Time: 0 minute

Servings: 4

Nutrition: Calories: 131 Fat: 7.3 g Carbs: 15 g Protein: 2.8 g

Ingredients:

- 3 slices of whole-grain bread
- 6 chopped cherry tomatoes
- ½ of sliced avocado
- ½ teaspoon minced garlic
- ½ teaspoon ground black pepper
- 2 tablespoons chopped basil
- 1 teaspoon balsamic vinegar

Directions:

- ❖ Place tomatoes in a bowl, and then stir in vinegar until mixed. Top bread slices with avocado slices, then top evenly with tomato mixture, garlic and basil, and season with black pepper.
- ❖ Serve straight away

110) Cream Cheese Spread

Preparation Time: 15 minutes

Cooking Time: 0 Minutes

Servings: 6

Nutrition: Calories 204 Fat 6.7g Carbs 7.3g Protein 4.5g

Ingredients:

- 12 ounces cream cheese, soft
- 1 big tomato, cubed
- ¼ cup homemade mayonnaise
- 2 garlic cloves, minced
- 2 tablespoons red onion, chopped
- 2 tablespoons lime juice
- Black pepper to the taste

Directions:

- ❖ In your blender, mix the cream cheese with the tomato and the rest of the ingredients, pulse well, divide into small cups and serve cold.

111) Sweet Carrots

Preparation Time: 10 minutes

Cooking Time: 10 minutes

Servings: 04

Nutrition: Calories 119 Total Fat 14 g Carbs 19 g Protein 5g

Ingredients:

- 2 cups baby carrots
- 1 tablespoon brown sugar
- ½ tablespoon vegan butter, melted
- A pinch of black pepper

Directions:

- ❖ Take a baking dish suitable to fit in your air fryer.
- ❖ Toss carrots with sugar, butter and black pepper in the baking dish.
- ❖ Place the dish in the air fryer basket and seal the fryer.
- ❖ Cooking Time: the carrots for 10 minutes at 350 degrees F on air fryer mode.
- ❖ Enjoy.

112) Italian Patatoes

Preparation Time: 15 minutes

Cooking Time: 40 Minutes

Servings: 4

Nutrition: Calories 122 Fat 11.6g Carbs 4.5g Protein 0.6g

Ingredients:

- 1/3 cup baby red potatoes
- 1 tablespoon Italian seasoning
- 3 tablespoons canola oil
- 1 teaspoon turmeric
- ½ teaspoon dried rosemary
- 1 tablespoon dried dill

Directions:

- ❖ Cut the red potatoes into the wedges and transfer in the big bowl. After this, sprinkle the vegetables with Italian seasoning, canola oil, turmeric, dried rosemary, and dried dill.
- ❖ Shake the potato wedges carefully. Line the baking tray with baking paper. Place the potatoes wedges in the tray. Flatten it well to make one layer. Preheat the oven to 375F.
- ❖ Place the tray with potatoes in the oven and bake for 40 minutes. Stir the potatoes with the help of the spatula from time to time. The potato fries are cooked when they have crunchy edges.

113) Lemon Leeks

Preparation Time: 10 minutes

Cooking Time: 7 minutes

Servings: 04

Nutrition: Calories 231 Fat 20.1 g Carbs 20 g Protein 4.6 g

Ingredients:

- 1 tablespoon vegan butter, melted
- 1 tablespoon lemon juice
- 4 leeks, washed and halved
- Black pepper to taste

Directions:

- ❖ Take a baking dish suitable to fit in your air fryer.
- ❖ Toss the leeks with butter and black pepper in the dish.
- ❖ Place the dish in the air fryer basket.
- ❖ Seal the fryer and Cooking Time: the carrots for 7 minutes at 350 degrees F on air fryer mode.
- ❖ Add a drizzle of lemon juice.
- ❖ Mix well then serve.

114) Tempeh Bit

Preparation Time: 15 minutes

Cooking Time: 8 Minutes

Servings: 6

Nutrition: Calories 88 Fat 2.5g Carbs 10.2g Protein 6.5g

Ingredients:

- 11 oz soy tempeh
- 1 teaspoon olive oil
- ½ teaspoon ground black pepper
- ¼ teaspoon garlic powder

Directions:

- ❖ Cut soy tempeh into the sticks. Sprinkle every tempeh stick with ground black pepper, garlic powder, and olive oil. Preheat the grill to 375F.
- ❖ Place the tempeh sticks in the grill and cook them for 4 minutes from each side. The time of cooking depends on the tempeh sticks size. The cooked tempeh sticks will have a light brown color.

115) Special Brussel Sprouts

Preparation Time: 10 minutes

Cooking Time: 10 minutes

Servings: 04

Nutrition: Calories 361 Total Fat 16.3 g Carbs 29.3 g Protein 3.3 g

Ingredients:

- 1-pound brussels sprouts, trimmed
- ¼ cup green onions, chopped
- 6 cherry tomatoes, halved
- 1 tablespoon olive oil
- Black pepper to taste

Directions:

- ❖ Take a baking dish suitable to fit in your air fryer.
- ❖ Toss brussels sprouts with black pepper in the dish.
- ❖ Place this dish in the air fryer and seal the fryer.
- ❖ Cooking Time: the sprouts for 10 minutes at 350 degrees F on air fryer mode.
- ❖ Toss these sprouts with green onions, tomatoes, olive oil, and pepper in a salad bowl.
- ❖ Devour.

116) Guacamole

Preparation Time: 15 minutes

Cooking Time: 0 Minutes

Servings: 8

Nutrition: Calories 200 Fat 14.5g Carbs 8.1g Protein 7.6g

Ingredients:

- ½ cup heavy cream
- 1 green chili pepper, chopped
- Pepper to the taste
- 4 avocados, pitted, peeled and chopped
- 1 cup cilantro, chopped
- ¼ cup lime juice

Directions:

- ❖ In a blender, combine the cream with the avocados and the rest of the ingredients and pulse well. Divide the mix into bowls and serve cold as a party dip.

117) Feta Asparagus

Preparation Time: 10 minutes

Cooking Time: 8 minutes

Servings: 04

Nutrition: Calories 201 Total Fat 8.9 g Carbs 24.7 g Protein 15.3 g

Ingredients:

- 2 pounds fresh asparagus, trimmed
- ½ teaspoon oregano, dried
- 4 ounces vegan feta cheese, crumbled
- 4 garlic cloves, minced
- 2 tablespoons parsley, chopped
- ¼ teaspoon red pepper flakes
- ¼ cup olive oil
- Black pepper to the taste
- 1 teaspoon lemon zest
- 1 lemon, juiced

Directions:

- ❖ Combine lemon zest with oregano, pepper flakes, garlic and oil in a large bowl.
- ❖ Add asparagus, pepper, and cheese to the bowl.
- ❖ Toss well to coat then place the asparagus in the air fryer basket.
- ❖ Seal the fryer and Cooking Time: them for 8 minutes at 350 degrees F on Air fryer mode.
- ❖ Garnish with parsley and lemon juice.
- ❖ Enjoy warm.

118) *Kalamata Bruschetta*

Preparation Time: 15 minutes

Cooking Time: 15 Minutes

Servings: 24

Nutrition: Cal 73 Fat 4.8 g Carbs 5.3 g Protein 2.1 g

Ingredients:

- 6 Kalamata olives, pitted, chopped
- 2 tablespoons green onion, minced
- 1/4 cup Parmesan cheese, grated, divided
- 1/4 cup extra-virgin olive oil brushing, or as needed
- 1/4 cup cherry tomatoes, thinly sliced
- 1 teaspoon lemon juice
- 1 tablespoon extra-virgin olive oil
- 1 tablespoon basil pesto
- 1 red bell pepper, halved, seeded
- 1 piece (12 inch) whole-wheat baguette, cut into 1/2-inch-thick slices
- 1 package (4 ounce) feta cheese with basil and sun-dried tomatoes, crumbled
- 1 clove garlic, minced

Directions:

- ❖ Preheat the oven broiler. Place the oven rack 6 inches from the source of heat. Brush both sides of the baguette slices, with the 1/4 cup olive oil.
- ❖ Arrange the bread slices on a baking sheet; toast for about 1 minute each side, carefully watching to avoid burning. Remove the toasted slices, transferring into another baking sheet.
- ❖ With the cut sides down, place the red peppers in a baking sheet; broil for about 8 to 10 minutes or until the skin is charred and blistered.
- ❖ Transfer the roasted peppers into a bowl; cover with plastic wrap. Let cool, remove the charred skin. Discard skin and chop the roasted peppers.
- ❖ In a bowl, mix the roasted red peppers, cherry tomatoes, feta cheese, green onion, olives, pesto, 1 tablespoon olive oil, garlic, and lemon juice.
- ❖ Top each bread with 1 tablespoon of the roasted pepper mix, sprinkle lightly with the Parmesan cheese.
- ❖ Return the baking sheet with the topped bruschetta; broil for about 1-2 minutes or until the topping is lightly browned.

119) *Epic Artichokes*

Preparation Time: 10 minutes

Cooking Time: 10 minutes

Servings: 04

Nutrition: Calories 119 Total Fat 14 g Carbs 19 g Protein 5g

Ingredients:

- 4 big artichokes, trimmed
- ¼ cup olive oil
- 2 garlic cloves, minced
- 2 tablespoons lemon juice
- 2 teaspoons balsamic vinegar
- 1 teaspoon oregano, dried
- Black pepper to the taste

Directions:

- ❖ Season artichokes liberally with pepper then rub them with half of the lemon juice and oil.
- ❖ Add the artichokes to a baking dish suitable to fit in the air fryer.
- ❖ Place the artichoke dish in the air fryer basket and seal it.
- ❖ Cooking Time: them for 7 minutes at 360 degrees F on air fryer mode.
- ❖ Whisk remaining lemon juice, and oil, vinegar, oregano, garlic and pepper in a bowl.
- ❖ Pour this mixture over the artichokes and mix them well.
- ❖ Enjoy.

120) *Seven Spices Beef (or lamb)*

Preparation Time: 15 minutes

Cooking Time: 10 Minutes

Servings: 1 Phyllo Pie

Nutrition: Calories: 299 Carbs: 53g Fat: 6g Protein: 7g

Ingredients:

- 1 lb. ground beef or lamb
- 1 medium yellow onion, finely chopped
- 1 tbsp seven spices
- 1 pkg. frozen phyllo dough (12 sheets)
- 2/3 cup butter, melted

Directions:

- ❖ In a medium skillet over medium heat, brown beef for 3 minutes, breaking up chunks with a wooden spoon.
- ❖ Add yellow onion, seven spices, and cook for 5 to 7 minutes or until beef is browned and onions are translucent. Set aside, and let cool.
- ❖ Place first sheet of phyllo on your work surface, brush with melted butter, lay second sheet of phyllo on top, and brush with melted butter. Cut sheets into 3-inch-wide strips.
- ❖ Spoon 2 tablespoons meat filling at end of each strip, and fold end strip to cover meat and form a triangle.
- ❖ Fold pointed end up and over to the opposite end, and you should see a triangle forming. Continue to fold up and then over until you come to the end of strip.
- ❖ Place phyllo pies on a baking sheet, seal side down, and brush tops with butter. Repeat with remaining phyllo and filling. Bake for 10 minutes or until golden brown.
- ❖ Remove from the oven and set aside for 5 minutes before serving warm or at room temperature.

DASH DIET

DESSERT

RECIPES

121) Graham Cracker Cheesecake

Preparation Time: 30 Minutes

Cooking Time: 90 Minutes

Servings: 12

Nutrition: Calories: 98kcal Carbs: 7g Fat: 7g Protein: 3g

Ingredients:

- 2 cups graham cracker crumbs (about 30 crackers)
- ½ tsp ground cinnamon
- 6 tbsps. unsalted butter, melted
- ½ cup sesame seeds, toasted
- 12 ounces cream cheese, softened
- 1 cup crumbled feta cheese
- 3 large eggs
- 1 cup of sugar
- 2 cups plain yogurt
- 2 tbsps. grated lemon zest
- 1 tsp vanilla

Directions:

- ❖ Set the oven to 350°F.
- ❖ Mix the cracker crumbs, butter, cinnamon, and sesame seeds with a fork. Move the combination to a springform pan and spread until it is even. Refrigerate.
- ❖ In a separate bowl, mix the cream cheese and feta. With an electric mixer, beat both kinds of cheese together. Add the eggs one after the other, beating the mixture with each new addition. Add sugar, then keep beating until creamy. Mix in yogurt, vanilla, and lemon zest.
- ❖ Bring out the refrigerated springform and spread the batter on it. Then place it in a baking pan. Pour water in the pan till it is halfway full.
- ❖ Bake for about 50 minutes. Remove cheesecake and allow it to cool. Refrigerate for at least 4 hours.
- ❖ It is done. Serve when ready.

122) Banana Smoothie

Preparation Time: 5 minutes

Cooking Time:

Servings: 1

Nutrition: Carbs: 34.1 Protein: 12.8 g Fats: 14 g Calories: 244

Ingredients:

- Almond butter: 1 tbsp
- Large banana: 1 frozen
- Fresh kale: 1 cup
- Unsweetened almond milk: ¾ cup

Directions:

- ❖ Add all the ingredients to the blender
- ❖ Blend to form a smooth consistency

123) Brandy cookie balls

Preparation Time: 20 Minutes

Cooking Time: 45 Minutes

Servings: 20

Nutrition: Calories: 294 Carbs: 44g Fat: 12g Protein: 3g

Ingredients:

- 4 cups of sugar, divided
- 4 cups of water
- 1 cup plus 1 tbsp. honey, divided
- 1 (2-inch) strip orange peel, pith removed
- 1 cinnamon stick
- ½ cup extra-virgin olive oil
- ¼ cup unsalted butter,
- ¼ cup Metaxa brandy or any other brandy
- 1 tbsp. grated
- Orange zest
- ¾ cup of orange juice
- ¼ tsp baking soda
- 3 cups pastry flour
- ¾ cup fine semolina flour
- 1 ½ tsp baking powder
- 4 tsp ground cinnamon, divided
- 1 tsp ground cloves, divided
- 1 cup finely chopped walnut
- 1/3 cup brown sugar

Directions:

- ❖ Mix 3 ½ cups of sugar, 1 cup honey, orange peel, cinnamon stick, and water in a pot and heat it for about 10 minutes.
- ❖ Mix the sugar, oil, and butter for about minutes, then add the brandy, leftover honey, and zest. Then add a mixture of baking soda and orange juice. Mix thoroughly.
- ❖ In a distinct bowl, blend the pastry flour, baking powder, semolina, 2 tsp of cinnamon, and ½ tsp. of cloves. Add the mixture to the mixer slowly. Run the mixer until the ingredients form a dough. Cover and set aside for 30 minutes.
- ❖ Set the oven to 350°F
- ❖ With your palms, form small oval balls from the dough. Make a total of forty balls.
- ❖ Bake the cookie balls for 30 minutes, then drop them in the prepared syrup.
- ❖ Create a mixture with the walnuts, leftover cinnamon, and cloves. Spread the mixture on the top of the baked cookies.
- ❖ Serve the cookies or store them in a closed-lid container.

124) Banana-Mango Smoothie

Preparation Time: 5 minutes

Cooking Time:

Servings: 1

Nutrition: Carbs: 73.1 g Protein: 10.5 g Fats: 18.7 g Calories: 486

Ingredients:

- Frozen mango chunks: 1 cup
- Almonds: ¼ cup whole
- Oat milk: ½ cup
- Frozen banana: 1 large sliced

Directions:

- ❖ Add all the ingredients to the blender
- ❖ Blend until smooth

125) Walnuts Balls

Preparation Time: 20 Minutes

Cooking Time: 45 Minutes

Servings: 10

Nutrition: Calories: 355 Carbs: 64g Fat: 7g Protein: 6g

Ingredients:
- 2 cups of sugar
- 1 cup of water
- 1 cup honey
- 1 ½ cups tepid water
- 1 tbsp. brown sugar
- ¼ cup of vegetable oil
- 1 tbsp. active dry yeast
- 1 ½ cups all-purpose flour, 1 cup cornstarch, ½ tsp salt
- Vegetable oil for frying
- 1 ½ cups chopped walnuts
- ¼ cup ground cinnamon

Directions:
- ❖ Boil the sugar and water on medium heat. Add honey after 10 minutes. cool and set aside.
- ❖ Mix the tepid water, oil, brown sugar,' and yeast in a large bowl. Allow it to sit for 10 minutes. In a distinct bowl, blend the flour, salt, and cornstarch. With your hands mix the yeast and the flour to make a wet dough. Cover and set aside for 2 hours.
- ❖ Fry in oil at 350°F. Use your palm to measure the sizes of the dough as they are dropped in the frying pan. Fry each batch for about 3-4 minutes.
- ❖ Immediately the loukoumades are done frying, drop them in the prepared syrup.
- ❖ Serve with cinnamon and walnuts.

126) Special Mango Smoothie

Preparation Time: 5 minutes

Cooking Time:

Servings: 1

Nutrition: Carbs: 27.2 g Protein: 10 g Fats: 15.1 g Calories: 270

Ingredients:
- Almond butter: 1tbsp
- Frozen mango chunks: ½ cup
- Banana: 1 small
- Flax seeds: 1 tsp
- Ground cinnamon: ¼ tsp
- Hemp seeds: 1 tsp
- Coconut milk: 1 cup beverage

Directions:
- ❖ Add all the ingredients to the blender
- ❖ Blend to form a smooth consistency

127) Vanilla Caramel

Preparation Time: 60 Minutes

Cooking Time: 60 Minutes

Servings: 12

Nutrition: Calories: 110 Carbs: 21g Fat: 1g Protein: 2g

Ingredients:
- 5 cups of whole milk
- 2 tsp vanilla extract
- 8 large egg yolks
- 4 large-sized eggs
- 2 cups sugar, divided
- ¼ cup 0f water

Directions:
- ❖ Preheat the oven to 350°F
- ❖ Heat the milk with medium heat wait for it to be scalded.
- ❖ Mix 1 cup of sugar and eggs in a bowl and add it to the eggs.
- ❖ With a nonstick pan on high heat, boil the water and remaining sugar. Do not stir, instead whirl the pan. When the sugar forms caramel, divide it into ramekins.
- ❖ Divide the egg mixture into the ramekins and place in a baking pan. Increase water to the pan until it is half full. Bake for 30 minutes.
- ❖ Remove the ramekins from the baking pan, cool, then refrigerate for at least 8 hours.
- ❖ Serve.

128) Strawberries-Orange Smoothie

Preparation Time: 5 minutes

Cooking Time:

Servings: 4 cups

Nutrition: Carbs: 25.2 g Protein: 15.5 g Fats: 18.6 g Calories: 462

Ingredients:
- Peanuts: 1 cup
- Almonds: 1 cup
- Strawberries: 6
- Orange: 1
- Pineapple: 1 cup chopped
- Water: 1 cup

Directions:
- ❖ Add all the ingredients to the blender
- ❖ Blend to form a smooth consistency

129) *Special Cake*

Preparation Time: 30 Minutes

Cooking Time: 90 Minutes

Servings: 12

Nutrition: Calories: 393 Carbs: 55g Fat: 15g Protein: 8g

Ingredients:
- 4 cups sugar, divided
- 1 tbsp. fresh lemon juice
- 1 cup of water
- 1 Tbsp. plus 1 ½ tsp grated lemon zest, divided into 10 cups
- Room temperature whole milk
- 1 cup plus 2 tbsps. unsalted butter, melted and divided into 2
- Tbsps. vanilla extract
- 7 large-sized eggs
- 1 cup of fine semolina
- 1 package phyllo, thawed and at room temperature

Directions:
- ❖ Preheat oven to 350°F
- ❖ Mix 2 cups of sugar, lemon juice, 1 ½ tsp of lemon zest, and water. Boil over medium heat. Set aside.
- ❖ Mix the milk, 2 Tbsps. of butter, and vanilla in a pot and put-on medium heat. Remove from heat when milk is scalded
- ❖ Mix the eggs and semolina in a bowl, then add the mixture to the scalded milk. Put the egg-milk mixture on medium heat. Stir until it forms a custard-like material.
- ❖ Brush butter on each sheet then arrange all over the baking pan until everywhere is covered. Spread the custard on the bottom pile phyllo
- ❖ Arrange the buttered phyllo all over the top of the custard until every inch is covered.
- ❖ Bake for about 40 minutes. cover the top of the pie with all the prepared syrup. Serve.

130) *Zucchini Smoothie*

Preparation Time: 5 minutes

Cooking Time:

Servings: 2

Nutrition: Carbs: 33.1 g Protein: 12.2 g Fats: 18.0 g Calories: 335

Ingredients:
- Coconut milk: 1 cup
- Peanut butter: 2 tbsp
- Frozen banana: 1 small sliced
- Frozen zucchini: 1/2 cup sliced

Directions:
- ❖ Add all the ingredients to the blender
- ❖ Blend to form a smooth consistency

131) *Carrot Smoothie*

Preparation Time: 5 minutes

Cooking Time:

Servings: 1

Nutrition: Carbs: 27.2 g Protein: 10 g Fats: 15.1 g Calories: 256

Ingredients:
- Frozen mango chunks: ½ cup
- Carrot: 1 small peeled and chopped
- Coconut milk: 1 cup beverage
- Ground cinnamon: ¼ tsp
- Ripe persimmon: ½ ripe
- Flax seeds: 1 tsp
- Almond butter: 1tbsp
- Hemp seeds: 1 tsp

Directions:
- ❖ Add all the ingredients to the blender
- ❖ Blend to form a smooth consistency

132) *Brandy Almond Cookies*

Preparation Time: 20 Minutes

Cooking Time: 50 Minutes

Servings: 20

Nutrition: Calories: 102 Carbs: 10g Fat: 7g Protein: 2g

Ingredients:
- 1 ½ cups unsalted butter, clarified, at room temperature 2 cups
- Confectioners' sugar, divided
- 1 large egg yolk
- 2 tbsps. brandy
- 1 1/2 tsp baking powder
- 1 tsp vanilla extract
- 5 cups all-purpose flour, sifted
- 1 cup roasted almonds, chopped

Directions:
- ❖ Preheat the oven to 350°F
- ❖ Thoroughly mix butter and ½ cup of sugar in a bowl. Add in the egg after a while. Create a brandy mixture by mixing the brandy and baking powder. Add the mixture to the egg, add vanilla, then keep beating until the ingredients are properly blended
- ❖ Add flour and almonds to make a dough.
- ❖ Roll the dough to form crescent shapes. You should be able to get about 40 pieces. Place the pieces on a baking sheet, then bake in the oven for 25 minutes.
- ❖ Allow the cookies to cool, then coat them with the remaining confectioner's sugar.
- ❖ Serve.

133) Pineapple-Orange Smoothie

Preparation Time: 5 minutes

Cooking Time:

Servings: 4 cups

Nutrition: Carbs: 12.2 g Protein: 2 g Fats: 0.2 g Calories: 48

Ingredients:
- Strawberries: 6
- Orange: 1
- Pineapple: 1 cup chopped
- Water: 1 cup

Directions:
- ❖ Add all the ingredients to the blender
- ❖ Blend to form a smooth consistency

134) Special Lemon Cake

Preparation Time: 30 Minutes

Cooking Time: 3 Hours

Servings: 24

Nutrition: Calories: 348 Carbs: 55g Fat: 9g Protein: 5g

Ingredients:
- 1 tbsp. unsalted butter
- 2 tbsps. all-purpose flour
- 1 cup ground rusk or bread crumbs
- 1 cup fine semolina flour
- ¾ cup ground toasted almonds
- 3 tsp baking powder
- 16 large eggs
- 2 tbsps. vanilla extract
- 3 cups of sugar, divided
- 3 cups of water
- 5 (2-inch) strips lemon peel, pith removed
- 3 tbsps. fresh lemon juice
- 1 oz of brandy

Directions:
- ❖ Preheat the oven to 350°F. Grease the baking pan with 1 Tbsp. of butter and flour.
- ❖ Mix the rusk, almonds, semolina, baking powder in a bowl.
- ❖ In another bowl, mix the eggs, 1 cup of sugar, vanilla, and whisk with an electric mixer for about 5 minutes. Add the semolina mixture to the eggs and stir.
- ❖ Pour the stirred batter into the greased baking pan and place in the preheated oven.
- ❖ With the remaining sugar, lemon peels, and water make the syrup by boiling the mixture on medium heat. Add the lemon juice after 6 minutes, then cook for 3 minutes. Remove the lemon peels and set the syrup aside.
- ❖ After the cake is done in the oven, spread the syrup over the cake.
- ❖ Cut the cake as you please and serve.

135) Green Smoothie

Preparation Time: 5 minutes

Cooking Time:

Servings: 1

Nutrition: Carbs: 49.2 g Protein: 12.9 g Fats: 19.9 g Calories: 392

Ingredients:
- Large banana: 1
- Ice cubes: 4
- Pistachios: ¼ cup
- Fresh spinach: 1 cup
- Rolled oats: 2 tbsp
- Unsweetened almond milk: ¾ cup

Directions:
- ❖ Add all the ingredients to the blender
- ❖ Blend to form a smooth consistency

136) Oats Pudding

Preparation Time: 10 Minutes

Cooking Time: 15 Minutes

Servings: 4

Nutrition: Calories 174 Fat 12.1 Carbs 3.9 Protein 4.8

Ingredients:
- 1 tablespoon lemon juice
- Zest of 1 lime
- 1 and ½ cups of almond milk
- 1 teaspoon almond extract
- ½ cup oats
- 2 tablespoons stevia
- ½ cup silver almonds, chopped

Directions:
- ❖ In a pan, blend the almond milk plus the lime zest and the other ingredients, whisk, bring to a simmer and cook over medium heat for 15 minutes.
- ❖ Split the mix into bowls then serve cold.

137) Chia Smoothie

Preparation Time: 5 minutes

Cooking Time:

Servings: 2

Nutrition: Carbs: 24.0 g Protein: 23.1 g Fats: 11.2 g Calories: 376

Ingredients:
- Unsweetened coconut milk: 1 cup
- Blackberries: ½ cup
- Unsweetened coconut flakes: ¼ cup
- Banana: ½
- Chia Seeds Protein Powder: 2 scoops

Directions:
- ❖ Add all the ingredients to the blender
- ❖ Mix well and pour to the glass

138) *Dates Quinoa*

Preparation Time: 10 minutes

Cooking Time: 15 minutes

Servings: 2

Nutrition: Calories: 125, Protein: 2 g, Carbs: 8 g, Fat: 9g

Ingredients:
- 1½ cups water
- 1 cup quinoa
- 2 cinnamon sticks
- 1-inch knob of ginger, peeled
- 1 cup plain Greek yogurt
- ½ cup dates, pitted and chopped
- ½ cup almonds (raw or roasted), chopped
- 2 teaspoons honey (optional)

Directions:
- ❖ Bring the water, quinoa, cinnamon sticks and ginger to a boil in a medium saucepan over high heat.
- ❖ Reduce the heat to a simmer and cover; simmer for 10 to 12 minutes. Remove the cinnamon sticks and ginger. Fluff with a fork.
- ❖ Add the yogurt, dates, and almonds to the quinoa and mix together. Divide evenly among 4 bowls and garnish with ½ teaspoon honey per bowl, if desired.
- ❖ Use any nuts or seeds you like in place of the almonds.

139) *Dates and Friends Smoothie*

Preparation Time: 5 minutes

Cooking Time:

Servings: 4

Nutrition: Carbs: 24.9 g Protein: 3.5 g Fats: 1 g Calories: 148

Ingredients:
- Raw pumpkin:175 g
- Cloves:1
- Nutmeg:1/8 tsp
- Dates: 4
- Banana:1
- Ground ginger:1/8 tsp
- Ground cinnamon:1 tsp
- Cashew milk:500 ml
- Ice: as per your need

Directions:
- ❖ Add all the ingredients to the blender
- ❖ Blend on high speed to make it smooth

140) *Almond and Cocoa Smoothie*

Preparation Time: 5 minutes

Cooking Time: 30 minutes

Servings: 2

Nutrition: Calories: 125, Protein: 2 g, Carbs: 8 g, Fat: 9g

Ingredients:
- ¾ cup almond milk
- ½ medium banana, preferably frozen
- ¼ cup frozen blueberries
- 1 tablespoon almond butter
- 1 tablespoon unsweetened cocoa powder
- 1 tablespoon chia seeds

Directions:
- ❖ In a blender or Vitamix, add all the ingredients. Blend to combine.
- ❖ Peanut butter, sunflower seed butter, and other nut butters are good choices to replace the almond butter

Chapter 9 - Dr. Cole's Full Energy Meal Plan – For Athlete

Day 1

2) Chickpea Multigrain Toast | Calories 337

23) Arugula Linguine | Calories 274

64) Greek Chicken | Calories 472

45) Green Hummus | Calories 296

103) Chickpeas Hummus | Calories 122

124) Banana-Mango Smoothie | Calories 486

Total Calories: 1987

Day 2

5) Grains Breakfast | Calories 339

25) Mexican Style Pasta | Calories 304

66) Piccata Style Chicken | Calories 406

47) Red and Yellow Salad | Calories 227

115) Special Brussel Sprouts | Calories 361

125) Walnuts Balls | Calories 355

Total Calories: 1378

Day 3

7) Monkey Cream | Calories 272

27) Chili Macaronis | Calories 312

67) Salmon & Pesto | Calories 316

50) Herbed Cream Cheese Toast | Calories 194

113) Lemon Leeks | Calories 231

128) Strawberries-Orange Smoothie | Calories 462

Total Calories: 1787

Day 4

12) Date & Bannana Under Zero | Calories 350

29) Wave of Shrimp and Quinoa | Calories 324

70) Cauli Quinoa with chili | Calories 414

54) Shrimp Salad | Calories 314

109) Bruschetta Fusion | Calories 131

129) Special Cake | Calories 393

Total Calories: 1926

Day 5

20) Blueberries & Barley Bowl | Calories 295

32) Tomato Shower Pasta | Calories 378

76) Trout & Shallots | Calories 344

56) Mahi-Mahi Jicama | Calories 320

107) Veggie Taco | Calories 187

135) Green Smoothie | Calories 392

Total Calories: 1916

Day 6

6) Eggs Tarte with Spinach & Feta | Calories 240

39) Sweet Potatoes Stuffed | Calories 393

78) Quinoa Burger with a Sweet Touch | Calories 290

58) Boneless Salad | Calories 340

110) Cream Cheese Spread | Calories 204

137) Chia Smoothie | Calories 376

Total Calories: 1843

Day 7

16) Asiago Frittata | Calories 199

30) Cucumber Noodles | Calories 408

80) Sweet Salmon | Calories 454

60) Awesome Shrimp Cocktail | Calories 580

134) Special Lemon Cake | Calories 348

Total Calories: 1989

Chapter 10 -   Conclusion

I hope this book of recipes will be useful to you in the long term, I remind you that the DASH diet is a diet proven by specialists from various medical disciplines, it is not just a fad or for aesthetic reasons, it will really make a difference in your life and your health.

The best medicine for our body is to take care of our diet, and if in addition to taking care of our health we can show off a better figure is the perfect deal.

Keep in mind that the portions that I include in each recipe must be careful so that the diet works properly and you get the most out of all the benefits it offers.

As a final tip, I suggest you write in your diary or in a notebook a note about how you feel before starting the diet, how you see your body, write down your weight, if you feel swollen or if you have heaviness, have any difficulty, in short your feelings in general, keep your notes and when you have at least two or three weeks of following this diet review it again and you will discover the changes that are already beginning to occur.

Much success and welcome to a healthier and happier life.

Lightning Source UK Ltd.
Milton Keynes UK
UKHW050632110621
385329UK00002B/295